THE
T·SHIRT
BOOK

THE T·SHIRT BOOK

JOHN GORDON AND ALICE HILLER

EBURY PRESS 🙰 LONDON

Published by Ebury Press

Division of The National Magazine Company Ltd

Colquhoun House

27-37 Broadwick Street

London W1V 1FR

8808229

ISBN 0 85223 637 9 (hardback)

       0 85223 642 5 (paperback)

Edited by Veronica Sperling and Heather Rocklin

Designed by Gordon Ollis Design

Photography by Topflyht Promotions

Picture research by John Gordon and Alice Hiller

Typeset by Systemset Composition, London NW2 2LD

Printed and bound in Spain by Cronion S.A., Barcelona

CONTENTS

IN THE BEGINNING

The T-shirt is the global garment of the 20th century. Whether as cult icons or consumer classics, their comfort, low cost and disposability make them as popular in the Third World as the First. American in origin, T-shirts started out as undervests and grew up through World War II, Hollywood and Rock 'n' Roll before hitting the mass market as the top half of the jeans revolution.

As walking billboards, T-shirts have been used to promote everything from world peace to Coca-Cola, while *Time* magazine snapped President Reagan with the slogan STOP COMMUNISM IN CENTRAL AMERICA. Anthropologists term this technique of letting your T-shirt do the talking the "new primitivism" and draw parallels between body painting in Polynesian cultures and T-shirt wearing in the First World.

Americans bought 1.8 billion T-shirts in 1986; but the crewneck single jersey classic only really took off as outerwear in the early 1970's. By then the shape had been around for nearly 100 years, having evolved out of late 19th century men's underwear and sportswear. In England, amateur boxers and rowers wore a regulation two button halfsleeve cotton 'zephyr' from 1880 onwards, and the Royal Navy ordered sailors to sew sleeves on their white tanktops.

The first recorded T-shirt dates from the 1899 US Navy Uniform Regulation. This specified a revolutionary "lightweight shortsleeve white cotton undervest" at a time when most men still wore shirts and drawers. These subsequently gave way to the one piece Union Suit, but it took another 20 years before athletic dress styles

The first recorded retail sale of a printed T-shirt was in a shop in Ann Arbor, Michigan in 1933.

and the spread of central heating in the 1920's began to establish the T-shirt in America.

Even so, they were slow to catch on. Doughboys had brought sleeveless French Army cotton vests back from the trenches of World War I, introducing the concept of coolness and comfort into American underwear, but the 1930's were a bad time for undervests. Clark Gable appeared without one in the 1934 film *It Happened One Night* and plain T-shirts could hardly compete with the brightly colored A-line vests that dominated the decade.

Meanwhile, T-shirts were beginning to be used as sportswear, principally by the athletic departments of universities who started producing flocked shirts for their teams. Michigan date theirs from the 1920's while UCLA followed suit in 1931. The 30's also saw the first promotional and souvenir shirts. The 1939 *Wizard Of Oz* film T is now highly prized by collectors, but back then the public were not so keen.

Printed tops, still a very new idea, took another 30 years to catch on, with the result that outside college campuses T-shirts continued to be seen primarily as underwear. Hanes, a major US underwear manufacturer, reveal they first started producing T-shirts in 1935 but found few takers. Had it not been for the intervention of the US military, this most unique of garments might well have disappeared without a trace.

Pearl Harbor is generally regarded as the turning point for Europe but it also proved to be a timely saviour for the T-shirt. America's entry into World War II produced 11,000,000 new recruits all requiring regulation underwear and in 1942 the US Navy issued their suppliers with the

The US Navy called T-shirts "T-Types". Sailors called them skivvies and took them back home after the war to mow the lawn in.

Union Underwear produced the first Fruit Of The Loom label T-shirt in 1948.

The "Quarter-sleeve" became official US Army Uniform in 1949.

C

F

G

D

E

5"

A

B

The Navy T-Type was described as "lightweight flat knit white cotton undershirt, high neckline, 5" sleeve with ¾" hem, ¾" band of self material stitched around the opening, ⅞" hem at bottom."

The US Army ran a three month test on the Navy T-Type in Camp Indian Bay, Florida between June and September 1944.

John Wesley HANES

SHAMROCK HOSIERY MILLS

Above: diagram accompanying the US Army's 1955 Military Specification for Cotton Quarter- **sleeve Undershirts. The document ran to 8 pages of detailed instructions on constructing the perfect T!**

first official specification for what they called the "T-Type".

Hanes would manufacture over 40,000 over the next three years while Union Underwear, the biggest producer of underwear products in the world and the army's major supplier, also started making them for the first time. They had been designed as vests, but the troops also wore their T-shirts outdoors against sunburn and off duty in the evenings. Although most were still plain, T's printed with the names of army camps and individual divisions became very popular.

T-shirts had acquired a certain combat glamor during the war and a generation of American males went home sold on what the army termed their "better appearance" and "greater sweat absorbtion under the arms". The postwar period saw T-shirts becoming America's No. 1 vest. While the conservative fashions of the day limited their potential as adult outerwear, kids were soon wearing printed T's featuring contemporary heroes like Joe DiMaggio, Davy Crockett and Roy Rogers.

The next milestone in T-shirt history came in 1951 when *A Streetcar Named Desire* hit the screens. Marlon Brando played Stanley Kowalski in a classic cap sleeve white model and anyone who saw his "sensual, unfeeling, mean, vindictive" performance also saw the T-shirt in a completely new light. Director Elia Kazan described the film as "the first non-sentimental picture we have ever made over here" and T-shirts gained rebel status overnight.

8

Right: **Marlon Brando as Johnny in** *The Wild One.* **Worn with Nazi inspired leathers, the black collar on his white T-shirt reinforced the visual symbolism in a film based on the 1947 Hollister (biker) Riots.**

Left and below: **too fast to live, too young to die: James Dean's death in 1955 guaranteed sartorial immortality for the white T/blue jeans combo.**

1953 saw them linked with juvenile delinquency and motor-bike gangs when Brando wore one in *The Wild One* and the 50's equivalent of punks took to wearing T-shirts with leather jackets and black jeans against a backdrop of grey suits and twinsets. Meanwhile the other major rebel hero of the 50's, James Dean, turned T-shirts into his offscreen sartorial trademark and this fact did not go unnoticed by the newly emerging generation of teenagers.

Hollywood had promoted the T-shirt as a fashion item and they began to become more visible as outerwear as the decade progressed. Older guys might only wear them to wash the car in but the younger generation teamed their T's with jeans, dungarees and Chinos. On the style front, plain was still tops but stripes began to creep in and by the late 50's the beatniks had launched the blue and white striped "French onion seller" look as classic intellectual gear.

Printed T-shirts, on the other hand, remained a specialist product. They had been accepted on the campuses and in the summer camps, and continued to be used in a small way as souvenir, promotional and novelty items. The most dynamic developments occured within the thriving hot-rod subculture. Dragsters started printing T-shirts with names of their cars – Red Demon, King Duster – and racing teams – the Rude Nights, Rebel Rockers – in the mid 50's.

Customizing was a key ingredient in the scene and the flames, dragons, and pinstripes that started out on cars were soon being airbrushed onto T-shirts. Surfers were quick to pick up the trend, while in England the 50's saw the first tentative use of printed T-shirts within specialist sports.

Fifty years down the line, T-shirts had become America's No. 1 undervest and were beginning to be worn as outerwear. Screen-printing was now sufficiently developed to allow small runs, while better inks meant anyone could do it. The following decade would see T-shirts taking hold outside their American homebase . . .

THE T-SHIRT REVOLUTION

In 1960, in England, printed T-shirts could be obtained exclusively through fabric printers who charged 9d a shirt and specified a six month delivery date.

Below right: Lord Kitchener's Valet: a swinging London store on Picadilly Circus.

Below: Mouse and Kelley's classic Grateful Dead logo.

Time magazine described the 1960's as "a decade dominated by youth". The period that spawned the mini-skirt also pulled T-shirts out of the closet and onto the street. Put in the spotlight by some of the best-looking bodies around – Brigitte Bardot was pictured in T-shirts from 1960 onwards, while Jean Seberg wore one in *Breathless* – they were worn by millions of women as sexy, casual outerwear for the first time.

Actresses apart, print was what got T-shirts noticed and by the time the public were ready to put pictures on their chests, the means existed to get them there cheaply and efficiently. America led the world, scoring a first with the invention of the plastisol transfer in 1963. Plastisol inks had been around since 1954, but the heat transfer gave T-shirts consumer appeal. People loved being able to pick a design and watch it being put on their shirts in a couple of minutes.

Early transfers featured basic cartoon-type artwork but the decade also saw major refinements in screen-printing. Surf culture was booming and inspired the first elaborate

multi-coloured T-shirts in the mid-60's. Artwork that started out being painted and airbrushed onto boards rapidly crossed over to shirts in both America and Australia. England, however, still had a lot of catching up to do both in terms of public acceptance and printing technology.

The Mods were the first UK subculture to make the T-shirt part of their wardrobe in the early 60's, introducing a long, colored, stripey model developed from cut-off rugger shirts. Carnaby Street boutiques picked up on the trend and SWINGING LONDON, GONK and LOVE T-shirts were all bestsellers in 1966. Printing was still a backstreet garage business however, and the only inks available were the water-based varieties which had to be heat cured – often in launderette driers.

Meanwhile, London led the world in youth fashion. New looks were emerging almost weekly and 1966 saw the birth of two major new T-shirt styles. Biba came up with a T-shirt mini-dress, while Chester Marton created the three button tie-dye classic. Plain T's were customized with DIY designs in iron-on vilene and by 1968 T-shirts were considered hip enough for the Government to run an anti-smoking campaign aimed at teenagers, featuring models in WE DON'T SMOKE T's.

Swirling psychedelic graphics with titles like DEEP SLEEP and SWEET DREAMS crossed from posters to T-shirts in the summer of '68. Humorous slogans were also popular. Typical of the period were the Canadian Novelty Shirt Co. Their "American Styled" shirts came pre-shrunk in 18 colors and cost 39s 11d. Slogans included GOBI DESERT CANOE CLUB, PLAYBOY UNIVERSITY and MOTHER'S WORRY, DADDY'S HEADACHE.

Left: 1970 saw T-shirt maxi dresses echoing the longer hemlines as designers started to explore the possibilities of cotton jersey as a cheap, high fashion fabric.

Above: the three button Grandpa vest: the quintessential 60's T-shirt was equally popular with rock stars and their fans.

Cotton-polyester blend T-shirts were introduced in America in 1965. Previously they had been 100% cotton.

Right: appliqués spilled over from jeans to T-shirts in the late 60's.

American inks first became available in England in 1967.

Inspired by West Coast hippy culture, 1967 had seen a looser look entering the fashion scene. Style-setting pop stars including Steve Marriott, Peter Frampton, Elton John, David Bowie and Mick Jagger were all spotted in T's. This official endorsement fuelled the transition from novelties to fashion items, and T-shirts' changing status was reflected in the new styles.

Three button "Grandpa vest" and tight cap-sleeves replaced the classic crewneck box T while the skin-tight long sleeve version became *the* shirt to print on. Psychedelic and pop art influences fused to produce bright, light-hearted designs featuring Mickey Mouse, Superman and GOD BLESS WOOLWORTHS. Tourists snapped up the new souvenir T's and football supporters showed equal enthusiasm for team shirts.

By the early 70's British T-shirts had become satin-appliqué, rhinestone-studded fantasies on purple, tangerine and green jersey that were a million miles from the plain white undervest of the 50's. Sold through boutiques, they swept into the mass market as the top half of the jeans revolution less than a decade after the first models went on sale in Carnaby Street.

In America the 1960's saw continuing growth within the college and promotional markets as major brand names like Budweiser started to appear on the cotton jersey billboards. Promo T's would only really take off in the early 1970's, however. The key developments of the decade came with the printed T-shirt's entry into counter culture.

City Authorities estimated there were 10,000 hardcore hippies resident in San Francisco by April '67, and the streets of Haight Ashbury exploded with psychedelic imagery. Posters and underground publications were the starting point for a graphic revolution that spilled over to T-shirts. Silk screen reached undreamt of heights as artists like Mouse and Kelley plundered a century of pop culture to produce T-shirts that incorporated Indian Braves, UFOs

Above: commemorative T-shirt sold to raise money for the *Oz* magazine obscenity trial at the Old Bailey in August 1971. Three editors of what the Establishment saw as the mouthpiece of permissive society were jailed on charges relating to the *Oz* 28 Schoolkids issue. John Lennon described the verdict as "disgusting fascism", while demonstrators protested outside the courtroom. The sentences were later suspended. Other T-shirts from this free-thinking, psychedelic and somewhat sexist publication included JAIL BAIT OF THE MONTH, THREE VIRGINS and A TYPICAL DETECTIVE-INSPECTOR . . .

14

Right: Wonder Workshop T-shirts distilled the flamboyance of the early 70's. Artists John and Molly Dove started the label in 1971. Their hand-printed designs had a major influence on T-shirt graphics. Sophisticated prints were realised through a pioneering use of photographic screens and photomontage techniques. The WILD THING Hendrix tribute was subsequently pirated round the world, while the rhinestones incorporated into the design sparked off a major craze.

British entrants in the 1968 Olympic Games were issued with an official T-shirt which featured a blue and red stripe and sew on patch against a white background.

and silent movie vamps into art nouveau graphics.

Robert Crumb's STONED AGAIN and KEEP ON TRUCKING became the visual anthems for a decade and in 1969 the first of the new imprinted T-shirts hit New York. Finn, who now owns The T-shirt Gallery, claims to have started the trend and his designs like the CND sign (made out of a woman with her legs apart with a man above her!) sold like wildfire. Rock promoters and bars wanted their own, and within a year T-shirts rocketed into the limelight.

Bands like The Grateful Dead lived in plain T's while Joe Cocker gave the tie-dyed style the ultimate seal of counter-culture approval when he wore it onstage in front of the 500,000 hippies at Woodstock. Meanwhile the T-shirt had become involved in changing the world. Peace signs, Viet Cong flags, clenched fists captioned with the word STRIKE and Women's Liberation slogans all sold through 'head shops' to a generation devoted to demonstrating against the war in Vietnam.

By September 1970 the printed T-shirt had swept across America and *Time* magazine reported that everyone from North Dakota farmers to Mrs David Rockefeller Jnr and Raquel Welch were "into the undershirt scene". Women wore them bra-less, slogans shouted LIBERATE MARIJUANA and SUPER ZAP THEM ALL WITH LOVE while the more conservative followers of fashion bought cartoon T's featuring Road Runner, Mickey Mouse, Batman and Superman in their millions.

Printed shirts had finally been accepted as universal outerwear. Most people still saw them as fashion novelties – but they wore them – and this shift in attitudes paved the way for the T-shirt boom of the 70's and 80's. Before long T-shirts would be used by everyone from Hell's Angels to multinationals, turning a medium that had evolved by accident rather than by design into a major industry. One of the first groups to pick up on the T-shirt's potential was the music business . . .

CHAPTER 3

IT'S ONLY ROCK AND ROLL

One of the rarest rock T-shirts has to be the BRYAN FERRY name shirt, which Bryan commissioned in a limited edition of one.

Next to World War II and Marlon Brando, rock has to be the best thing that ever happened to T-shirts. The perfect way for fans to show their loyalty, T-shirts gained a new level of credibility in this marriage made in heaven. The Winterland Productions merchandising company is one of America's largest suppliers of screenprinted sportswear and their $80 million sales total for 1986 is proof of just how popular the medium has become.

Rock T-shirts range from the blasphemous to the banal. Dead Kennedy's followers are TOO DRUNK TO F*** while pop fans go for full color portraits. Whatever form the image takes, wearing someone's name, face or logo on your chest is the ultimate compliment you can pay them. Where music is concerned, it implies an identification not just with the sound, but also with the personality of the group or performer.

Worn in America since the early 70's, printed rock shirts came to power when popular music was at its most influential. Record sales had reached an all-time high and albums were out-selling singles for the first time. Their roots, however, lie in the 1960's. T-shirts became walking billboards but more importantly, this period was when The Beatles pioneered the concept of using album covers as a way to link music with visual images.

Between 1968-72, this idea would develop, via posters, into the T-shirts that allowed fans to become active participants in the musical experience. By then, simple printed T-shirts were being used to identify road crews at concerts, while musicians like Frank Zappa had already been wearing plain models onstage for some time.

Rock festivals including Woodstock and Strawberry

Left: the 70's witnessed a major evolution in rock shirt designs. The classic 1972 Rolling Stones T was one of the first big sellers—but seems very basic compared with the all-over prints that had become standard by the end of the decade.

Fields picked up on the trend, but these T's were small runs produced for staff or as promotional items. The only shirts originally available to fans were one-offs as in a *New Musical Express* advertisement from May '68. Captioned "Your Favourite On A Tee Shirt", it invited fans to send in photos of pop starts, actors and heroes which would be printed on a "quality, washable Tee Shirt".

One of the first real rock shirts came into being in 1969 when a Grateful Dead fan had Jerry Garcia's face silkscreened onto a T. Alan Elenson wore his brainchild to see the band at New York's Fillmore East venue and was promptly beseiged by Deadheads. An initial print run of 300 sold out immediately, and by the summer of 1970 Alan's "Out Front" company had become a nationwide operation turning out bootleg tributes to the bands of the day.

Bands started out being pleased to feature on the most credible billboards around, but before long unlicensed entrepreneurs were selling up to 20,000 $3·00 shirts on a 50 date tour. A new force had entered the rock arena and it was time to get involved. The first official T's were organized by bands via their management or local promoters although some worried that selling T-shirts would be seen as selling out.

Once again the Grateful Dead played a key role. In 1972 they started selling their T's in the lobby of promoter Bill Graham's Winterland hall in San Francisco while they were playing. The response was "overwhelming". Bill Graham decided to take T-shirts on the road and set up Winterland Productions to handle what was the first official concert merchandise.

Licensed T-shirts reached the East Coast in 1973 when

Below and top left: loyal patronage by artists from the Boomtown Rats to Blondie has made the T-shirt an integral part of the rock 'n' roll lifestyle.

the Allman Brothers' assistant manager, Ira Sokoloff, put their HELL YEAH slogan onto cotton jersey. Printed over a black and white photo of the band against the Confederate flag, it was followed by MUSHROOM, EAT A PEACH and BROTHERS AND SISTERS. These became four of the top American rock shirts in the early 70's.

The Rolling Stones' lolling tongue design was also a huge seller and their 1972 tour is credited with establishing the T-shirt as regulation concert wear in America. Before long everyone from David Bowie to Carole King could be seen on the chests of young Americans. England was a different matter.

Few companies had the automatic machines necessary for big runs and commercial printing in Britain was still years behind America. One or two bands, including Hawkwind and Mott The Hoople, started organizing their own tour shirts through independent studios but the major market revolved around teeny pop bands like David Cassidy, The Bay City Rollers, The Jackson Five and Donny Osmond.

Rock T's only became widely available in Britain around 1978 thanks to the combined forces of punk and heavy metal. Punk introduced a subversive element with prints like the Sex Pistols' GOD SAVE THE QUEEN plus safety pin – and gave T-shirts rebel appeal for a generation out to shock.

Simultaneously Whitesnake and Thin Lizzy were doing the first mass produced, complex, quality graphics. Meanwhile, superior American single jersey T-shirts were beginning to replace the old interlock cotton model. A tendency to shrink and become shapeless had made the latter a less than desirable garment! T-shirts became compulsory top wear for followers of both styles, hitting the mass market as new wave bands started to dominate the charts.

Heavy metal acts also introduced the first real volume sales in the UK. When Led Zeppelin played at Knebworth Park in '78 they sold out of 25,000 T's in one weekend. By the late 70's T-shirt sales were at record levels on both sides of the Atlantic. Pirates were flooding the market with

Right: reggae and Two-tone are among the galaxy of musical styles to have found graphic expression on T-shirts.

Impresario extraordinaire Malcolm McLaren used the medium to spread the word about his bands, as with the Bow Wow Wow shirt shown here.

Many acts are content to decorate T-shirts with adaptations of their record covers, although some designs are more individual. An example of a shirt evolved under the artist's supervision is the HAVE GUITAR WILL TRAVEL design from tireless performer Billy Bragg.

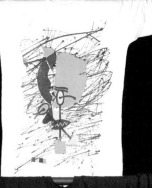

BOW WOW WOW

SEE JUNGLE! SEE JUNGLE! GO JOIN YOUR GANG YEAH, CITY ALL OVER GO APE CRAZY

BILLY BRAGG

HAVE GUITAR WILL TRAVEL

EIN StÜRZE NDE NEU BAU TeN

WE ARE ALL PROSTITUTES

Thomas Dolby

POSITIVE NOISE

MAGAZINE
THE CORRECT USE OF SOAP

PINK FLOYD

BIG COUNTRY

THE HUMAN LEAGUE

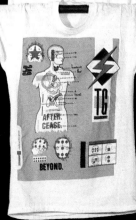

AFTER. CEASE.

BEYOND.

THE BOTTOM LINE

A TEN POINT GUIDE TO T-SHIRT SALES . . .

1. **Boys buy more T-shirts than girls.**

2. **Chart success does not always relate to T-shirt sales.**

3. **Heavy metal sells more T-shirts than any other single musical style proportionately. Bands like Agnostic Front, Iron Maiden and Poison seldom reach the Top Ten and their fans wear their T-shirts as a statement of solidarity.**

4. **The same rule applies to cult acts like The Clash, The Smiths, The Mission, King Kurt, Sisters of Mercy, The Cure and, of course, The Grateful Dead.**

5. **Cult sales can vanish overnight, however, if a band crosses over into the mainstream. Fans who consumed huge numbers of T-shirts during Adam Ant's wilderness years stopped buying T's as soon as he made it.**

6. **Artists who *wear* T-shirts *sell* T-shirts. Heavy metal is an obvious example but this is equally true of T-shirt phenomena like the Beastie Boys and U2.**

7. **Major tours guarantee massive T-shirt sales but this popularity does not always last — by late '86 some retailers said they could hardly give away Bruce Springsteen T's.**

8. **Pop is a dodgy area for T-shirts. Fans may buy them in huge quantities when bands tour/top the charts but a large number of pop fans are both female and fickle and lack the fidelity of male metal supporters.**

9. **Fans are also very specific about what they want. Cult supporters tend to go for subversive imagery (eg The The's INFECTED which featured the devil masturbating in rubber gloves) while metal concentrates on epic graphics (Whitesnake's serpent with naked woman is a classic). Pop fans, however, like a nice full color picture of their star. AHA reportedly lost out on a lot of sales by going for a more mysterious look but Duran got it right with a series of five photos of the band which became the best-selling UK shirts when they came out.**

10. **Abba and Barry Manilow seldom sell T-shirts . . .**

Winterland, the San Francisco-based international merchandising company can print 120,000 shirts a day for their roster of over 75 entertainers ranging from Madonna to The Monkees.

Below: **the Boss's butt: Bruce Springsteen's unique 1986 tour shirt . . .**

bootlegs and alternative designs and the major licensing companies decided to move in and clean up . . .

In America, Winterland and The Great Southern Company led the way in what *Rolling Stone* magazine termed "The T-shirt Wars". The Great Southern Co. instituted the first National Restraining Order on July 3 1980 against a bootlegger selling Judas Priest T's. That year saw Winterland systematically and successfully persuading all the major bootleg companies to start stocking licensed product or get out.

Britain followed suit in 1982 when bands including The Who, The Police, Motorhead and Iron Maiden banded together with Mobile Merchandising (Britain's major merchandising company) and the majority of rock and pop T-shirts are now licensed. Artists are paid royalties on their T-shirts and can demand substantial advances. Michael Jackson's UK rights went for £50,000 – but such deals rest on contracts which can become invalid if an act changes line-up or fails to tour.

T-shirts were tailor-made for rock. Casual and

comfortable, the classic crewneck box T is the perfect medium for the message. Merchandising accounted for $20,000,000 of the $50,000,000 gross on the Rolling Stones' 1981/2 tour and is now a multimillion dollar business. At the end of the day, however, it still rests on individual fans stating their personal loyalties. Nothing can do this better than a T-shirt . . .

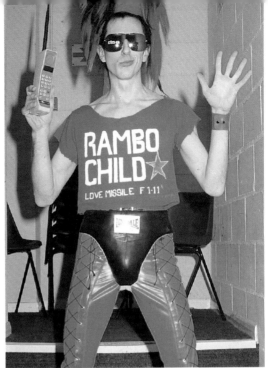

Psychologists have noted that much of the hearing takes place through the skin, and one theory puts rock shirts' popularity down to the fact that they help the sensual appreciation of high amplified electronic music by exposing more than just the face and ears!

T-TYPES

Rock and Pop T-shirts divide into four principal categories:

TOUR SHIRTS: *The* rock T-shirt, bought by fans in huge quantities at concerts — Madonna sold one every six seconds on her Virgin Tour. The best are printed with the tour dates and have a status value through the "I was there" element which also makes them an evocative souvenir to be worn long after the event.

RETAIL SHIRTS: Sold primarily in record shops, these T's were originally bootlegs and tour over-runs. Now supplied by licensed merchandise companies, they frequently feature a separate design to tour shirts.

PROMOTIONAL SHIRTS: Produced by record companies to help market a new record, these are generally given away to key media personnel such as DJ's and journalists. As such they are considerably more exclusive than either of the previous categories. An early example is the limited edition of RED ROSE SPEEDWAY T's for Paul McCartney's 1973 solo album. A maximum of five were given out in each major American city.

IN HOUSE: The rarest shirt of all and virtually impossible to get hold of unless you are actually involved in a specific band/company/project. The graphics company, Assorted Images, were commissioned to produce a design for Simon Le Bon's yacht *Drum*. The resulting T-shirt featured an Inca-style eagle on the front and a map of the world tracing the route on the back. Printed in full color for the general public, it was also produced in black and white for crew members.

Autograph, the first Russian rock band to perform live in the west, wore black Russian made T-shirts printed with a star and sickle for their press pictures.

Above and right: **Vicki Mocket had been responsible for some of the most distinctive music based T-shirts to emerge in the 80's although the rock genre is still largely male-dominated.**

The 12″ square pack many shirts are now sold in originated in America and was designed so T-shirts could be racked like albums.

Above: a Girlschool member pays tribute to one of the original heavy metal bands while Marilyn goes for the model look.

THE HARD SELL

Promotional T-shirts' colors are carried over from product packaging to produce an instant subconscious association.

Below: a Presidential promotion.

Promotional T-shirts are both the cornerstone and founding fathers of T-shirt culture. Not only does their market share by far exceed that of any other style, but they were also the first printed T-shirts and instigated many technical innovations. The first decorated T's to be worn in any quantity, promos pioneered the medium as a means of advertising and an expression of wearer loyalty which has since been exploited by everyone from rock bands to political parties.

T-shirts are now used to advertise just about anything. A Californian funeral parlour claimed it was THE ONLY WAY TO GO on a black T; Live Aid and U.S.A. for Africa shirts spread the word and raised millions for the fight against famine; upmarket Chanel models are designer status symbols. In contrast, the first promotional T-shirts were considerably more low key and originated on American college campuses in the late 1920's.

Still seen by most people as vests, they were flocked with the names of athletic teams. Sweaters had been used to identify players since 1860 but low price lightweight T-shirts were much better suited to the job. Michigan University, UCLA and Washington were among the first to have their own T-shirts and by 1957 Velvasheen (who specialized in the educational market), was printing 50,000 college shirts a year.

The late 50's saw most college bookstores stocking a range of T-shirts and this crossover from the track to more general wear was reflected in the designs. College names, official insignia and team motifs had become classics but they started to be joined by more individual promotions like

HARVARD . . . THE WASHINGTON UNIVERSITY OF THE EAST which Washington brought out in 1960 to publicize their academic achievements.

Subsequently adopted by high schools and summer camps, educational promos were worn throughout America long before other styles became available and played a major role in transforming the way Americans perceived the medium. The college connection made printed T-shirts 'acceptable' as adult wear. The next stage came with the T-shirt's exploitation by mainstream advertisers.

Small scale advertising on T-shirts had also started out in the 1930's but promotions were usually for local enterprises such as garages or as gimmick novelties. Commercial shirts featuring product logos developed alongside billboards and premiums such as matchboxes. Targeted at teenagers and children they only really got going in the 1960's when the major companies became involved.

Budweiser was one of the first in 1965. Television advertising which featured the Bud beer label on clothing, the bottom of a swimming pool and a basketball blackboard resulted in a huge demand for T-shirts. Loyal beer drinkers wanted to identify themselves with their favourite drink and wearing the label on their chest was the perfect way to do it.

This period also saw the new franchise operations which had sprung up in the wake of the 1956 Interstate Highway Act using T-shirts to develop consumer loyalty. The McDonalds' kid told people to TAKE LIFE A LITTLE EASIER, Howard Johnsons had SAM THE CLAM and everyone from *Rolling Stone* readers to Dick Clark's

Anheuser-Busch, Budweiser's parent company, sold more than 780,000 T-shirts in 1986, 50% up on the previous year.

Above and right: promotional T-shirts are designed to build awareness of the brandname and maximise consumer loyalty by combining colors and styling from the product packaging with current advertising themes.

Above: Adidas T-shirts were originally worn by professional athletes and came onto the leisure market in 1980. Early models featured a straightfor-ward logo, but by the late 80's a wide range of fashion-orien-tated colors and styles had become available.

''The objective of the Promotional Products Group is to extend and enhance beer brand awareness via quality U.S. manufactured merchan-dise.'' Anheuser-Busch, Budweiser's brewers.

American Bandstand viewers could now be seen wearing their particular preferences with pride.

By 1969 Coco-Cola were billing their NATIONAL THIRST ELIMINATOR T-shirt as THE COMPLETE PUT-ON. Advertised in specialist car magazines, it featured a Coke bottle on wheels. Motoring was also a major theme in early British promos. Racing sponsors commissioned team shirts to be worn on and around the track in the 1960's but the primitive printing industry combined with British reserve to prevent the medium taking off until the 1970's.

Ironically the first examples to be worn widely were all bootlegs. One hundred percent pure label artwork from Southern Comfort, Extra Stout Guinness and even Moet & Chandon champagne were all part of a craze that swept through British boutiques in the early 1970's. Levi's logo and the famous Playboy bunny were two major non-alcoholic hits, after which the legal copyright holders had no choice but to get in on the act.

Pepsi then became LIPSMACKINTHIRST/ QUENCHINACETAST/ INMOTIVATINGOOD/ BUZZINCOOLTALKIN/ HIGHWALKINFASTLIV/ INEVERGIVIN/ COOLFIZZIN while Coke was IT! Meanwhile, milk's declining share of the British soft drinks market saw the Milk Marketing Board hitting back with a

Right and below: the actress, the model and the judge: Pamela Stevenson, Jo Latham and Lord Denning demonstrate the T-shirt's potential for self-promotion.

The UCLA initials first appeared on a T in 1931. Now UCLA & UCLA Bruins are Federally Registered trademarks in the USA, UK and 20 other countries and worldwide licensed sales of UCLA products total $10,000,000

The SLO, or self-liquidating offer, involves manufacturers offering branded T-shirts to consumers at wholesale prices.

Promotional T-shirts are usually targeted at a specific age range or interest group and made available on a limited basis via on pack or point of sale mail order offers.

Right: Nancy Reagan and friends at an anti-drugs rally.

Left: the Jamaican Tourist Board's biggest assests —this poster has graced travel agents' offices since the 1970's.

range of T's including I'M A CRAZY MILK DRINKER.

By the mid 70's everyone from Greenpeace to Adidas was saying it on cotton blend and the stage was set for the first of the major nationwide T-shirt campaigns. JAWS' American release in 1975 was advertised on a record 200,000 official T-shirts. Three years on, Bacardi Rum shifted 250,000 shirts in the UK alone while those loveable blue Smurfs, as promoted through Nat Benzols' garage forecourts, became a major T-shirt phenomenon.

Subsequent kids' fads like E.T. and Pac Man have all proved to be short and sweet – seldom lasting over six months but clocking up massive sales. The profit factor has also been a key in the development of adult promotions. T-shirts have evolved from being giveaways to become major money spinners and companies have responded by setting up separate divisions to cope with the demand.

From Coke's 1970 Peace Sign through to Budweiser's 1987 Spuds MacKenzie, promotional T-shirts have derived their phenomenal appeal from the combination of hard sell brandname packaging with ultra-current graphics. Frequently subsidised and sold to the public at little over cost price, they enable people to define themselves through the products they consume and represent a radical breakthrough in non-verbal communication!

Jean Seberg wore a New York Herald Tribune shirt in Goddard's 1959 film "Breathless".

Right: **English National Opera and Opera North have both recognised the value of promotional T-shirts. The Orpheus in the Underworld T was designed by Gerald Scarfe for the ENO.**

Left and right: **further examples of the promotional T-shirt's versatility.**

The first ever plastisol transfer incorporating a photograph, appeared on a promotional T-shirt for the Tastee fast food company in 1970 and featured a hot dog . . .

Above: adult entertainment: an unlikely video casting director and dancers at the Crazy Horse Club.

Right: spot the imposter: Hermes bootlegs became street fashion status symbols in 1987 although the copyright holders failed to appreciate the free publicity.

Below: Jimmy Connors in one of the world's most popular promos. The design may be basic but a meal at the Hard Rock Café is not complete without the purchase of one of their T-shirts.

Bottom: Elton John and Bjorn Borg on holiday.

32

Above:
upmarket shirts: readers of *The Face* magazine were able to order T-shirts featuring a selection of its greatest covers.

Far right (middle): the Bad God design was created by artists Gilbert and George for a limited edition beer label.

CHAPTER 5

IF YOU LIVED IT, WEAR IT

34

"For the average person born outside of America, they don't have a hope in hell of getting here. The closest thing they'll ever come to the US is a TV show or a T-shirt. Everyone wants American T-shirts. By wearing them they can feel part of what's going on here." Marc Polish, who exports out-of-date American T-shirts round the world very successfully.

T-shirts have been printed as souvenirs since the 1930's in America. While the designs are seldom exceptional, souvenir shirts serve a very important function. Unlike rock or promotional shirts, their popularity depends on people's own interests rather than somone else's product, and the statements they make are much more personal.

The 1982 Royal Wedding T's may have been crass, but wearing one showed you thought Charles and Diana were great. Live Aid T-shirts said you cared about Africa's starving millions and allowed people to become actively involved, even if they had only watched the show on television.

From the Mount St Helena's DUST IN THE WIND T, recording the volcanic explosion, to the holiday maker's I GOT DRUNK IN BLACKPOOL, these T-shirt trophies express a human need to commemorate which stretches back to prehistoric man. The first hunters wore the skin, antlers and teeth of their prey and the combat factor is present in the military's use of the medium.

World War II generated wartime mementoes on both sides. American soldiers bought up shirts printed with their platoons' insignia and names of army camps, while the German versions featured the eagle and swastika emblems. The British Armed Forces now commission T-shirts for the troops. Their Falklands T-shirts have become prized souvenirs for those who served there, as have those printed for the US Peace-keeping Forces in Beirut.

The vast majority of souvenir T-shirts are of a non-combative nature, however. Initially developed alongside promotional T-shirts, they frequently combine the two functions. Walt Disney sold the first Mickey Mouse T-shirts as souvenirs at Disneyland, simultaneously promoting the newly opened theme park.

Early American college T-shirts were also sold as souvenirs and everything from the classic OXFORD UNIVERSITY and HARVARD T's, to the more recent IDONTGOTO UNIVERSITY are still very popular with tourists. By the early 1950's American resorts like the FABULOUS HAMPTONS had started selling T-shirts. In England the CARNABY STREET sign T became an instant bestseller in the 60's.

The 70's saw T-shirts becoming universal outerwear and every holiday destination from ATLANTIC CITY IS A LOT OF CRAP AND BLACKJACK AND SLOTS AND FUN to I HAD IT IN JAMAICA got in on the act. Peruvian peasants

Left: transatlantic sniping: a British I Hate N.Y. T-shirt from the Assorted Images design group . . .

WOODSTOCK FESTIVAL T-shirts were originally produced in a staff edition of 10. Thousands sold after the event.

Right: I was there . . .

Below: variations on the koala theme from Australia's thriving T-shirt industry.

Above right: massed banks of souvenir T-shirts have become a standard feature of cities round the world.

THIS T-SHIRT SAVES LIVES

Below: Live Aid, Wembley Stadium: 13 July 1985.

LIVE AID sold so many T's in England that it exhausted manufacturers' supplies of white T-shirts for the rest of the summer, while RUN THE WORLD took two million shirts out of the UK market alone. Together with the original FEED THE WORLD, these T's became personal souvenirs of epic events. By wearing them, punters not only stated their support but also demonstrated an active involvement as part of the shirt price was donated to Band Aid.

Charities have traditionally used T-shirts as fund-raising and promotional tools but they are at their most effective when combined with specific events. Winterland report that sales of T-shirts for LIVE AID, HANDS ACROSS AMERICA, U.S.A. FOR AFRICA, AMNESTY INTERNATIONAL and FARM AID all raised millions of dollars for their respective causes in America.

Meanwhile FASHION AID scored a real first with T-shirts from leading designers including Calvin Klein, Georgio Armani and Yves St Laurent. Many had never worked in the medium before and these unique creations were all sold after the event to raise money for the cause. The last word on the effectiveness of these new style charity T's had to come from the Duchess of Kent, however. She chose to wave Katharine Hamnett's LETS STOP CHILDREN DYING in place of her speech at the live show.

On-the-day Live Aid shirts can be identified by a spelling error in the list of artistes performing. Nik Kershaw is spelt Nike.

Run The World took two million white T-shirts out of the UK market.

QUEEN BANS
FERGIE T-SHIRT
Fury over Palace decision

Sun Royal special

BURT WOOS PRISCILLA!

Today's lucky numbers—Page 18

Palace bans wedding T-shirts

By John Young

Buckingham Palace became embroiled in controversy yesterday over a decision to ban the use of royal portraits and emblems on T-shirts and other articles of clothing to commemorate the wedding of Prince Andrew and Sarah Ferguson.

With all due respect Ma'am...
HOW CAN YOU OBJECT TO THIS?

THE QUEEN'S advisers must be a funny lot, as wedding fever sweeps the nation over the nuptials of Prince Andrew and his lovely young bride Sarah Ferguson, they have decreed that nobody in Britain should manufacture T-shirts showing the happy couple.

CONGRATULATIONS JULY 23 1986

"It is the Queen's decision...she doesn't feel they are a suitable place for royal photographs"

Row over ban on Fergie T-shirts

Textile firms slam 'killjoys'

By DANNY McGRORY

BRITAIN'S textile firms are furious because the Queen ban barred them from cashing in on the royal wedding.

T-shirt plea

Mr Bill Boggon, secretary of the Leicester Knitting Industry Association, is considering asking the Queen to reconsider the ban on T-shirts bearing pictures of Prince Andrew and his fiancée, Miss Sarah Ferguson.

POLICE SUSPENDED OVER ANGEL KILLING:

Torso charge

Above, left and below: **Queen Elizabeth II's refusal to allow the pictures of the happy couples to be used on T-shirts received extensive press coverage—but failed to have much impact on sales.**

Below right: **Gavin Beaumont from Splash, Britain's major souvenir shirt company, defying the ban on Charles and Di T-shirts. They may have been in bad taste but patriotic punters and monarchy hungry tourists didn't care.**

print T-shirts on the side of roads in the Andes, Detroit has become THE WORN CITY, Texans sell IF YOU'RE GOOD AND SAY YOUR PRAYERS, WHEN YOU DIE YOU'LL GO TO TEXAS.

T-shirts now rank second only to tans as proof you went there, and last considerably longer. This popularity has turned two designs into global classics. MY MUM WENT TO . . . AND ALL SHE BOUGHT ME WAS THIS LOUSY T-SHIRT sells to English speaking tourists round the world, while I ♥ N.Y. is simple enough to rise above language barriers.

Now printed everywhere from Perth to Paris, the design was created by Milton Glaser, America's leading graphic designer. Few souvenir T's have such distinguished origins.

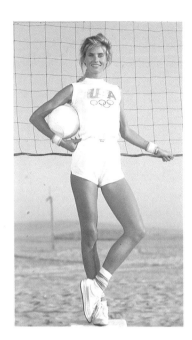

Hanes interview 125 printed T-shirt wearers each month. They have discovered that the median age of the average American T-shirt wearer is 34. More than half have had college education and 25 per cent are professionals.

Above right and right: shared memories: whether it's the last night at the Proms or Hands Across America, everyone wants a tangible reminder of a special event.

Opposite page, top and bottom: the Financial Times special was created for an employee leaving Saatchi & Saatchi, while Duran Duran spotted the cartoon of Princess Diana *(bottom row, far right)* in a newspaper.

The majority are produced by individual entrepreneurs without official sanctions—as was the case with the 1982 British Royal Wedding T's.

Guidelines from the Lord Chamberlain's Office excluded textiles, other than head scarves and wall hangings, from featuring pictures of Charles and Diana or the royal arms or cyphers. Fortunately this "in good taste" ruling carried no legal power and gaudy T-shirts sold briskly to everyone who wanted a memento of the "Wedding of the Century".

The 1976 American Bicentennial was another major T-shirt hit, but lesser events also sell large numbers of T-shirts. The Camp David Begin/Sadat summit, Comet Kahoutek in 1973 and Halley's Comet in 1986 all combined the once in a lifetime factor with high media coverage, which made a commemorative T essential.

The last solar eclipse inspired TOTAL FREAK and DO IT IN THE DARK T's. Sporting epics also sell shirts—loyal Muhammad Ali fans paid homage to their hero with the I WAS THERE, ZAIRE, SEPTEMBER 24, 1972 fight shirt. The 77–78 Tutankhamen Exhibition was seen by millions and inspired a rash of pun T's including LOVE MY MUMMY and KEEP YOUR HANDS OFF MY TUTS, although the humour in the CHERNOBYL EUROPEAN TOUR 1986 T was double-edged.

Space shuttle T-shirts sold by the thousands of dozens to everyone who wanted a personal record. After the 1986 Challenger disaster the patriotic Roger That company brought out a KEEP IT FLYING shirt. The lest we forget factor is also present in the Viet Vet designs which range from POW MIA to I WAS KILLING WHEN KILLING WASN'T COOL. From rock tours to Run The World, the message is: if you lived it, wear it!

TERRORVISION

♪ Tasty Tasty Very Very TASTY

GIVE US A KISS !!!

IN CASE OF EMERGENCY

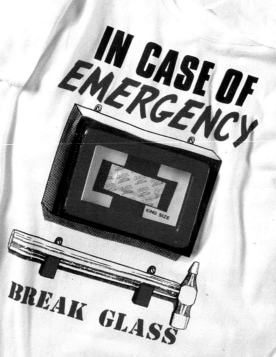

BREAK GLASS

DR PHILBYS

WORM TABLETS

ANYTHING GOES

Above: braille T-shirts were at their peak in the sexually liberated 70's.

Printed T-shirts were originally perceived as novelties, and their transition to mainstream fashion produced a boom in off-beat designs. Cheap enough to be bought on impulse, novelty T-shirts can be funny, libelous, or just bizarre. The most extreme shirts are almost unwearable, but the humorous slogans and images which started in the 60's continue to be bestsellers.

Early novelties announced membership of the OLYMPIC NECKING or the GOBI DESERT CANOEING teams. Current parodies of the college and state pride genre include designs like F.A.R.T.S. UNIVERSITY and EROTIC, NEUROTIC or PSYCHOTIC STATES. Simple prints gain a new dimension when the shirt is folded. Two lines of letters meet in the middle to become SC**W YOU. IF YOU CAN'T TAKE A JOKE has EXCUSE ME, F**K YOU printed on the inside.

The first really creative novelties appeared in the early 70's. Scratch 'n' Sniff T's featured everything from dill pickle jars to strawberries, each with their own aroma. Braille and Name and Phone Number T-shirts were tailor-made for extroverts. Cyclists had SAFE T's printed with a fluorescent orange hazard triangle. Beer drinkers could buy RING AROUND THE NAVEL shirts with a coaster for prone drinking.

T-shirts which re-interpret brand names and personalities have also become very popular. Americans reacted to the hostage crisis by turning the Ayatollah Khomeni's face into a road sign with a red circle and line through, while pornographic bootlegs give cartoon characters from Popeye to the Mister Men instant X Rating. Subverted company logos

Left: 3D T-shirts are supposed to have originated in Australia. These liquid latex creations are really only suitable for extroverts with strong stomachs . . .

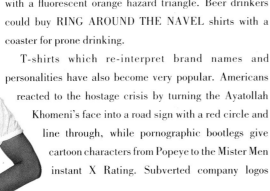

Left: the front and back of a one-off T-shirt commissioned by popstar Boy George in response to HRH Princess Margaret allegedly having called him a tart. The face on the bust is the Princess's and George wore his sartorial comment to a reception both were attending.

Below: an angler's dream: hanging textile fish enliven this American novelty.

include McDonalds/Marijuhana, while KENTUCKY FREUD CHICKEN T's are for gourmet intellectuals.

Make believe is also a major novelty theme. Why bother to get dressed up when you can slip into a Tuxedo T complete with bow tie and dress shirt? Alternately strip down to basics with a skeleton shirt. Illusion prints date from the mid 70's, but hardcore exhibitionists of the 80's can go one step beyond thanks to the advent of 3D T's.

Blood splattered axe handles and green worms stick out from shirts which have elevated bad taste into an art form. Novelty T's may be tacky and irreverent, but the major manufacturers turn over millions of dollars each year—and their success is proof that literally anything goes on a T-shirt.

Above and left: just about anything is game for T-shirt take-offs and the results are often more popular than the real thing. Miami Mice was one of the best selling T-shirts in Britain during the summer of 1986, while the University variations are perennial favorites.

Left, above left, above right: part of the range of T-shirts available from the Philadelphia T-Shirt Museum.

THE ATHLETIC SUPPORTER LTD.
24435 Halstead Road   Farmington Hills, Michigan
Toll Free 800-521-6500   in Michigan call (313) 474-6000
All designs © 1978-1986 The Athletic Supporter Ltd

Left, below and above right: illusion T-shirts hit the commercial mainstream in the mid 70's when fake tuxedos and cleavages were the ultimate in sartorial wit. Ten years on illusion shirts continue to flourish.

Right: getting it off your chest: the humour is seldom subtle but T-shirts have become the perfect way of stating your position on a very diverse range of subjects.

THE SPORTING CONNECTION

The major manufacturers of surf shirts such as Ocean Pacific pride themselves on their GRAPHIC ACCURACY. Surfers are featured in poses which look impossible but are in fact taken from photos.

***Opposite page:* Michael Roberts, British *Vogue's* design director, spent the winter of 86/7 in California working on paintings and photographs which became the basis for these distinctive T-shirts, captioned with surf slang.**

In 1976 only 25% of Americans owned printed T-shirts. By the mid 80's this figure had risen to nearly 70%. This spectacular increase can be attributed in part to the T-shirt's entry into the activewear market. Fitness is fashionable and specially printed T-shirts feature sports ranging from surfing and body building to hang gliding.

Active T's combining evocative graphics with snappy captions are the perfect way to advertise your sporting achievements—although they are also popular with armchair athletes. Surveys reveal that while the average American now owns six printed shirts, genuine "activists" tend to have upwards of 25 sporting T's in the closet!

The sporting connection has been a key element in the success of T-shirts since the 1930's, and the first non-campus printed sports shirts first appeared back in the 1950's. Official bodies, such as the National Amateur Body Building Association in England, distributed simple initialled shirts to their members, but the real activewear breakthrough came originally from the hot rod culture.

Enthusiasts started out wearing their team names on their T's, and soon got into explosive airbrush designs based on custom car artwork and monster themes. By the early 60's they had become major scene fashion items. Unfortunately fire marshals objected to the fumes and flammability of the oil based paints, and the transfers that replaced them lost the early graphic dynamism.

Meanwhile, surfers had begun to co-ordinate their boards with their T's by airbrushing competition pinstripes on both. More elaborate designs developed following the West Coast psychedelic explosion during the second half of the decade.

Multicolored images were hand painted and airbrushed onto boards and shirts, and by the early 70's screen printing had become standard.

Surfing was booming and specialist companies like Ocean Pacific and American Silk Screen started printing fantasy shirts featuring sunsets, flowers and the names of surfing paradises like Hawaii. Epic surf poses were also bestsellers. By the end of the decade hard-edged New Wave graphics had fused with the more romantic hippy originals.

Surf had taken over from hot rod as the activewear trailblazer, opening up the market for other sporting T's. It has also had a major influence on T-shirt shapes and was responsible for pioneering both the four button Berry T and the big baggy model in the 60's. Surfers lived in T's and were unable to move freely in the tight, skimpy fashion shirts of the period.

Both these styles have subsequently become 80's T-shirt classics while the surfing look has become increasingly fashionable. Lines like Ocean Pacific are now sold round the world in fashion outlets as well as sports shops, but the inspiration still comes exclusively from the beach and many of the major surf shirt companies are based in Southern California.

All Ocean Pacific's designers surf, and this is reflected in their washed out pastel prints of surfing traditions—like the T's and trunks strung out to dry between two surfboards at the end of the day. Classic wave riding poses continue to be big sellers, while in England Michael Roberts' Iron Surfer shirts feature surfing slang with cartoon images.

OP turned over $40,000,000 in 1986. While surf remains their major market, wind surfing and skate

Above: hardcore American surf shirts by Surfzoids, distributed in the UK by Alder.

"By wearing a T-shirt which associates a person with high quality products in a youthful lifestyle, he or she tells the world, 'I'm active'. We've found there are real activists and those who just suit up with a couple of trendy T's."... Kirk Beaudin, President, Hanes Printables.

boarding are both starting to feature heavily on T-shirts. Skate boarding in particular has become a very dynamic area, having developed from a kids' novelty in the 70's to become a fully fledged subculture with its own music, magazines and fashions.

Like surfers, skate boarders live in T-shirts, but their designs are considerably wilder. Demented graphics in acid colors reflect an urban sport based on concrete. Skulls and rats are favorite motifs for skaters who tune in to thrash metal and punk music. Some of the best T's feature designs from illustrators who specialize in board artwork.

Skate and surf T's have grown out of their respective subcultures and combine high profile glamor with street credibility. Since the mid 70's the more traditional sports have also inspired large numbers of T's. Skiers wear THINK SNOW, FREE STYLE, HOT DOG, GET IT TOGETHER, body builders prefer humorous designs or the names of famous gyms, while scuba diving has inspired detailed prints of exotic tropical fish.

Anglers can say they have fished in the fishing capital of the world, backpackers boast they have scaled the Tetons. T-shirts' comfort and freedom of movement make them perfect sportswear, while printed graphics allow wearers to identify their interests and refer to their achievements. The future looks good for an industry set to grow and grow . . .

Specialist sports shirt printer American Silkscreen sold 16,000 dozen T-shirts in 1982. In 1986 their total was 60,000 dozen.

Far right: hardcore skate shirts sold through shops like London's Slam City Skates, and the Texan Zorlac firm; and the watered down imitations (inset) for the mass market.

was sponsored by a bridal house.

The first Japanese Miss Wet T-Shirt

Right and far right: customized shower cabinets complete with disco lights have taken over from the jugs and buckets used to moisten contestants in early Wet T-Shirt competitions.

Las Vegas claimed to have held the biggest-ever Wet T-Shirt contest. It was divided into three categories, namely: FLAT IS BEAUTIFUL, BIG IS BEST, and NICEST CHEST IN THE WEST.

TEASE SHIRTS

From Marlon Brando through to Jacqueline Bisset, T-shirts
have been inextricably linked with sex. Whether in glossy
calendars or Wet T-Shirt competitions, it is a return to their
underwear roots that gives T-shirts this erotic appeal. They
now rate second only to conventional lingerie in glamour
photography, but T-shirt titillation was originally an
all-male preserve.

Brando's T-shirt was used to convey his animal-like
sexuality in *A Streetcar Named Desire*. Soaked with sweat
and nearly torn off at one point, the T-shirt showed his
muscled torso to perfection. White T's became an essential
part of the clean cut, athletic look that was a major theme in
postwar gay pin ups; while James Dean was an object of lust
for both sexes in his trademark T.

Brigitte Bardot, at her peak as a sex kitten, was among
the first to show that women could look sexy in T-shirts when
she took to wearing them in the early 60's. The combination
of bra burning and skin tight fashion shirts reinforced the
point, while the addition of printed slogans made the
message explicit.

Sexual liberation at its
most rampant inspired
everything from A HARD
MAN IS GOOD TO FIND

Left: evidence
of the T-shirt's
successful
penetration
into the
glamour
market.

and I THINK I COULD FALL MADLY IN BED WITH YOU to SEX IS LIKE SNOW . . . YOU NEVER KNOW HOW MANY INCHES YOU'LL GET OR HOW LONG IT WILL LAST. Meanwhile a more silent, not to say dumb, form of T-shirt seduction was flourishing in glamor photography.

This revolved around adding water to a plain T, worn bra-less, and reached its apex in 1977 with Jacqueline Bisset's memorable appearance in *The Deep*. Critics compared her wet T-shirt sequence to Marilyn Monroe's subway vent shot, while the film became a major American box office hit and Wet T-Shirt contests blossomed.

Originally conceived as garage promotions, they enjoyed brief but massive popularity in the States before being relegated to pornographic subculture. Elsewhere, however, Wet T competitions have become alternative beauty contests. The UK based Miss Wet T-Shirt runs to 150 heats

and features specially designed shower cabinets.

The format has been exported as far afield as Iceland and Japan, while the now universal practice of contestants customizing their T-shirts with scissors has resulted in spin-off ripped T-shirt competitions. Heterosexual exploitation may be hogging the headlines, but gay sexuality is expressed in underground T-shirts featuring homo-erotic imagery.

Cotton jersey lacks the automatic eroticism of black leather or silk, but worn wet and tight, it interacts with the human torso in a way that is nothing less than magical. Nearly half a century of association has bonded the link between sex and the T-shirt to the extent that, when the *News Of The World* interviewed a girl who claimed to have slept with Bob Geldof, they devoted several paragraphs to the revelation that he wore T-shirts in bed!

A student was banned from an exam for wearing an Aids inspired T-shirt with the slogan TRUST ME–I'M A CONDOM and only allowed back in after he had turned it inside out.

Above and top: whether campaigning or commenting, T's expressed the public's varying reactions to AIDS during the summer of 87.

Right: homo-erotic T's are very popular within the gay subculture.

Jacqueline Bisset gained instant notoriety from *The Deep* but was unhappy about the way in which her wet T-shirt image had been exploited. She told *Oui* magazine "I was caught in a shot that does not portray the context of the scene I was doing at the time".

Right: the born again morality of UK Today's T-shirt: based on a WWII Government poster it warns against VD— and is just one of a very diverse spectrum of sexual obsessions covered on T-shirts.

Above and left: sadomasochist bondage T-shirts cater for those with a need to shock.

Right and far right: whether it's pornographic subversions of kids' cartoons or plain blue jokes, anything goes as far as a certain section of the T-shirt buying public is concerned...

THE PROPAGANDA WARS

She just thinks she does

RUN THE WORLD

Right:
mainstream
American and
British
politicians
take T-shirts
far less
seriously than
their Third
World
counterparts.
The resulting
designs,
produced
during
election
campaigns,
tend to be
very basic.

**Nixon's
one-time Vice
President,
Spiro Agnew,
was the first
politician to
demand
royalties for
the use of his
face on
T-shirts. A
Columbus,
Ohio firm paid
him $2500
which was
subsequently
donated to
charity.**

"Some of the kindest people have the most strange appearance. You can't tell their politics by what they look like. You might be able to tell by what they've got printed on their T-Shirt but not by what they look like."
Margaret Thatcher, *Smash Hits*. 25.3.87.

T-shirts represent total sartorial democracy. Political prints from RIGHT ON RONNIE to WE SURVIVED THE 1986 PHILIPPINE REVOLUTION have become a global medium. Reuters Agency announced the appearance in Chinese markets of T-Shirts printed with the saying of Mao Tse-Tung in March 1967, and wearable propaganda is a major feature of life in post-revolution Iran.

Mainstream parties, disenchanted factions, and pressure groups everywhere use T-shirts to put their message across. Bigger than the button badges and more personal than the posters which preceded them, they allow individuals to state their personal affiliations or concerns —Margaret Thatcher's supporters backed her bid for Prime Ministership with PUT A WOMAN ON TOP FOR A CHANGE.

US activists wore IMPEACH NIXON and the first American political T-shirts were equally direct. The earliest example at The Smithsonian Institute dates from the 1948 Dewey-Truman Presidential race. DEW IT WITH DEWEY, together with the 1952 I LIKE IKE, the 1960 KENNEDY FOR PRESIDENT and the 1964 WE'D VOTE FOR LBJ, came exclusively in child sizes, however.

Adult versions became available in the mid 60's following the printed T-shirt's crossover into outerwear. By 1976 they were sufficently established for the Federal

Election Commission to ban the Democratic Committee of Georgia from printing Carter's and Mondale's faces on T-shirts.

They were said to represent an "illegal contribution to the electoral campaign". Such scruples seem ridiculous in countries where the political hard sell is conducted through sophisticated television campaigns. They could, however, be considered valid in the Third World where American shirts are major status symbols and propaganda is less developed.

Thousands of Zimbabweans saw Robert Mugabe's face for the first time on the VOTE Zanu PATRIOTIC FRONT T-shirt, prior to his victory in the 1980 elections. The Zanu shirts were printed in the UK, but both British and American custom printers report delivering orders in excess of 50,000 shirts to African nations, and these are often given away free to entire villages.

T-shirts have also become powerful tools in the fight against apartheid in South Africa. Cape Town police banned all T-shirts regardless of their slogans in January 1986. Anyone who contravened the order faced up to 10 years imprisonment or a fine of R20,000. Forced to step down in the face of public ridicule, police often make demonstrators take off T's like TROOPS OUT!

Slogans from FREE NELSON MANDELA and STOP KILLING INNOCENT PEOPLE to those supporting organizations like the UDF and COSATU are also forbidden in South African schools. Meanwhile, overseas sympathizers wear their support on their chests with shirts like the Anti-Apartheid Movement's portraits of freedom fighters or the ANC's official range.

**Union Jack T's
started out as
a 60's novelty
but by 1985
had assumed
fascist
connotations
in England.
The National
Council for
Civil Liberties
reported that
a York
University
student was
denied the
platform to
speak because
he was
wearing one.**

Below: the
1986
Philippine
Revolution
produced a
wealth of
T-shirts which
combine
no-nonsense
messages with
evocative
images. It's
the perfect
way of
presenting
politics to the
people.

Right:
politically
inspired T's:
European
Son's
Exploding
Kennedy
earned
smashed-in
shop windows
in The States.

Right:
Solidarity
leader Lech
Walesa
outside a
preview of the
film *Man of
Iron,* which
was directed
by Wajda, a
fellow Pole.

53

Right: protest
shirts employ
powerful
graphics to
make their
point.

Above: Israeli
Kahane
supporters in
Kach Party
T-shirts.

Left:
Divisional Commissioner of Police, Brigadier Chris Swart, cited this TROOPS OUT T as an example of the type of clothing banned.

Above left and left: **these South African T's received global coverage after Cape Town Police used emergency regulations to ban them in January 86. The ruling forbade the display of anything on which ''any viewpoint of a political nature or in relation to any system of government or constitutional policy is expressed, advocated or propagated.''**

The ultimate example of T-shirt Totalitarian-ism has to come from a Caribbean island with a population of 5000. Following an order of an equal number of T-shirts by one party, their election results became a foregone conclusion.

1987 saw popstars including Terence Trent D'Arby modelling 'designer' fund raising shirts from Artists Against Apartheid. Protest T's are becoming increasingly fashionable, but they first surfaced in the American anti-war movement of the 1960's, and by the 70's were being used by causes ranging from gay pride to environmental pressure groups.

Early US shirts sported the Viet Cong flag or bore pointed comments like FLY THE FRIENDLY SKIES OF CAMBODIA. The 1970 IT'LL BE A GREAT DAY WHEN OUR SCHOOLS GET ALL THE MONEY THEY NEED AND THE AIRFORCE HAS TO HOLD A BAKE SALE TO BUY A BOMBER is still selling, while QUESTION AUTHORITY is an evergreen theme.

Current ideological warrior wear continues to reflect the state of the nation. In America IT'S 10PM. DO YOU KNOW WHERE YOUR MARINES ARE? is superimposed over Marines creeping onto a map of Central America. A drawing of the White House bears the caption SEND IN THE CLOWNS . . . DON'T BOTHER THEY'RE HERE.

Martin Luther King quotes are cotton jersey classics. OUR SCIENTIFIC POWER HAS OUTRUN OUR SPIRITUAL POWER. WE HAVE GUIDED MISSILES AND MISGUIDED MEN is as valid today as it was when he said it. Now used by the anti-nuclear lobby, it expresses a concern which has been present on T-shirts since the CND sign crossed over from badges to shirts in the 60's.

British 1987 CND T's state U.S. BASES THE ENEMY WITHIN and BIG BOMBS SMALL PLANET. Americans make their point with messages ranging from the straightforward YOU CAN'T HUG YOUR KIDS WITH

Socialist singer Billy Bragg was mobbed when he performed in a Yuri Gagarin T-shirt in Moscow.

Right: Art-O-Matic produced this range of six T-shirts for Artists Against Apartheid and the International Anti-Apartheid Movement in 1987.

SOUTH AFRICAN T's

Government Gazette.

Pretoria, 26 June, 1986.   Schedule B.

"Prohibition on possession of certain articles or objects.

4. No person shall be in possession of . . .

(c) any uniform, part of uniform, T-shirt, flag, banner or pennant on which the name of any organization mentioned in Schedule C is depicted."

UDF spokesman Naseegh Jaffer said: "It is the height of absurdity. It seems the government is not only scared of the people's protest and power but also of the clothes we wear."

The Federation of Conservative Students at the extreme right wing of the British Conservative Party brought out a HANG NELSON MANDELA T.

Below: Paul Simon concert —Zimbabwe's largest multi-racial gathering.

NUCLEAR ARMS to the caustic NUCLEAR WAR . . . THERE GOES MY CAREER!, while the mushroom cloud comes with a cartoon style THAT'S ALL FOLKS!

Humor has also become a major ingredient in feminist shirts. The hardcore clenched first of the early 70's has given way to T's like HE'S PRETTY BUT CAN HE TYPE? featuring two Victorian gentlemen. Clouds illustrate WOMEN HOLD UP HALF THE SKY and GOD IS COMING AND IS SHE PISSED is set against a raging storm.

Alternative politics represent an ongoing theme in protest T-shirts but volume sales are generated by specific campaigns. LONDON SUPPORTS THE MINERS was just one of many shirts to come out of the 1984 British Miners' Strike. Across the Atlantic, American farmers make their point with slogans like RAISE LESS CORN AND MORE HELL: SAVE OUR FAMILY FARMS.

60's and 70's political T-shirts were mainly worn by committed compaigners. In 1984 designer Katharine Hamnett made world headlines when she wore a 58% DON'T WANT PERSHING T to meet Mrs Thatcher at Downing Street. Her designer slogans mean style conscious radicals can now state their position with T-shirts whose message has been sweetened by their entry into the fashion sphere.

Marxism Today's Clothing For Autonomy range includes THE FORWARD MARCH OF THE PROLETARIAT in full color. Their GORBACHEV T is billed as "the ultimate democratic fashion accessory" and part of the proceeds from their VIVA NICARAGUA design go to a Nicaraguan school. Meanwhile the British Labour Party's Jobs and Industry Campaign saw UK designer politics entering the mainstream.

Major parties seldom organize national T-shirt campaigns but Labour decided to present "the party's stance against unemployment in the most immediate way — by putting it on the backs of the young people it most directly concerns". T-shirts by four of London's fashion leaders even had the unique distinction of being officially launched by Labour Leader Neil Kinnock at the House of Commons.

Strictly for optimists: the American made ISRAEL-PALESTINE T featuring an Arab ploughing with two oxen and the caption SHARE THE LAND HARVEST THE PEACE.

Right: **David Bailey's photo provides powerful ammunition for LYNX's anti-fur trade T. The BOYCOTT! T refers to the Philippine Elections.**

LYNX

It takes up to 40 dumb animals to make a fur coat.
But only one to wear it.

Below: LYNX's '87 Roar of Protest collection *(bottom row)*, by Cathie Felstead, Hilary McManus and Lo Cole. Widely advertised, they exemplify the increasingly professional use of T's by pressure groups.

T-shirt trivia: alternative 1987 British Election T's included VOTE TACTICALLY from Katharine Hamnett. Spitting Image adapted her black type for I'M THE KIND OF BASTARD THAT VOTES TORY and other more libellous designs.

CHAPTER 10

SHOCK TACTICS

"T-shirts were the pinnacle of everything, they were seen everywhere." Malcolm McLaren. Punk rock hit Britain in late 1976 and was hailed by the *Daily Mail* as "the sickest seediest step in a rock world that thought it had seen it all". In fact it was a logical reaction both to the pompous excesses of glam rock and the worsening economic climate. Unemployment was rising with young people the worst-hit and "No future" became the catchphrase of a generation.

Bands and fans came together at London's all-punk Roxy venue. By the time it was shut down, after just three months in March 1977, the two minute thrash had become the basis for a movement. The Sex Pistol's *God Save The Queen* became the fastest selling single of the year when it was released that May. Anti-music and anti-fashion ruled OK, while T-shirts were reborn as sartorial shock tactics.

Ripped and held together with safety pins, printed with offensive images or scrawled with DIY obscenities, they rapidly became official punk uniform along with bondage strides, mohair sweaters and safety pins. Jamie Reid's GOD SAVE THE QUEEN T spelled out the message and generated headlines like the 1977 "JUBIPUNK—SEX PISTOL 'PIN UP' ROCKS PALACE". The ensuing text detailed the nation's outrage:

"Royal circles were rocking with horror last night at this Jubilee 'souvenir' produced by the Sex Pistols pop group. The punk rockers are offering a £3 T-shirt bearing a portrait of the Queen—with a safety pin through her lips. Guitarist Steve Jones said: . . . "We all think it's a bit of a laugh" . . . But Buckingham palace was far from amused. A spokesman said sternly: 'We think it is in deplorable taste.'"

Punk's musical roots may have been American but the shocking shirts were UK grown. Their genesis came about through Sex Pistols' Svengali Malcolm McLaren. Together with his partner Vivienne Westwood, he had been experimenting with the medium since 1971 — when the couple took over London's Kings Road shop that would later become Seditionaries, the mecca of punkcouture.

Malcolm and Vivienne started customizing shirts with everything from chicken bones to studded bicycle tyres, toilet chains, torn holes and cigarette burns. By 1975 they had already created many of the designs that would become punk classics. In the meantime, the premises had been rechristened Sex, and was selling their first 'zip across the tits' T's, together with black leather and rubber models.

Sex also stocked a range of bizarre fetishistic clothing, including leather bondage masks like the one worn by the Cambridge rapist. Printed on a T with the caption IT'S BEEN A HARD DAY'S NIGHT, this effectively initiated the concept of offensive T-shirt graphics. Malcolm and Vivienne then moved into exposing explicit, under the counter images on T-shirts, and their two cowboys, naked black rugby player and under-age nude Adonis later became major punk Ts.

Malcolm was simultaneously working with the Sex Pistols, and in March 1976 conscripted designer Jamie Reid into the project. Jamie had developed his cut up and photomontage techniques with Sophie Richmond at the campaigning Suburban Press; he now applied the blackmail lettering and anarchic style to Pistols' artwork. Originally used on handbills and flyposters advertising live gigs, this

Above and left: the genesis of the punk shirt: Malcolm McLaren and Vivienne Westwoods' first T's are preserved behind glass at the World's End shop. The chicken bone ROCK T was created for Alice Cooper in '71. The originals are collectors' items and virtually impossible to purchase at any price.

Right: Vivienne Westwood's classic punk design, photographed by Nick Knight for *The Face* magazine.

PRETTY IN PINK

NOT SO PRETTY IN PUNK

BONI

Brando notwithstanding, Richard Hell claims to have invented the torn punk T-shirt.

Sid Vicious caused an outcry when he wore a Swastika T in a Jewish area in France.

was also translated into T-shirts.

One of the first was for the 1976 ANARCHY IN THE UK single, on which the Sex Pistols' logo and song title were framed by a torn Union Jack, held together with safety pins. Meanwhile Malcolm and Vivienne's DESTROY took T-shirt outrage to the limit. The design combined an upside down crucifix, a postage stamp head of the Queen cut to look as if she had been beheaded, and a large dayglo swastika!

T-shirts had entered the punk vocabulary and fans responded by creating their own. Pink Floyd T's were defaced with I HATE written over the band's name in felt tip pen, while customizing became a major theme. Scrawled obscenities vied with band names like THE CLASH and THE DAMNED while the shirts themselves were ripped or slashed to look like knife cuts. By 1977 specially printed shirts had started to become available.

John and Molly Dove at Kitsch 22 did some of the first. Their dayglo leopard and tiger prints were universally copied and became *the* punk T, while shirts like the blow up Xerox of Johnny Rotten's face and Nazi Union Jack in black and red further defined the punk T style. Kitsch 22's collaged, all over prints also provided inspiration for the small companies who started up to print band shirts for punk fans.

Nazi regalia was an early theme—Sid Vicious was very keen on the swastika—but the political implications rapidly became too heavy for all but the most ardent neo-fascists. Adam Ant's fans promoted sexual deviancy with his range of powerful bondage illustrations. Major mass market styles revolved around rough and ready images like the EXTRA POWER CLASH shirt with its washing powder lettering over a photo of the band.

Some of the best band shirts came from the Fifth Column co-operative. Typical of the new breed of printers is that the designers shared an art school background, their large, multicolored shirts were printed by hand using techniques they had pioneered. Fifth Column T-shirts included Robin Richard's X-Ray Spex range based on singer Poly Styrenes'

John and Molly Dove designed their classic dayglo tiger print as an anti-fur trade protest in 1969 and resurrected it for punk.

Left: Kitsch 22 shirts by the Doves. The face belongs to Jordan, Malcolm McLaren's shop assistant, famed for going to work in rubber corsets and other fetish wear.

Left: Sid Vicious tabloid obituary became an instant bestseller after his death, and is now a T-shirt classic.

Above: 80's versions of the punk T style for die-hard fans. The Siouxsie Sioux face is by Artistique et Sentimentale, who have grown from their punk roots to become one of Britains most successful cult shirt companies.

Above and above right: **Robin Richards punk T's featuring X-Ray Spex and the Sex Pistols.** Subsequent Two-Tone and Gothic movements produced the black and white checks and skull motifs respectively.

Right: the original cut-out collage style and blackmail lettering live on in Jamie Reid's T-shirts for '87.

''Punk wasn't shrouded with mystery, the imagery was simple, direct. People could come up with their own statements.'' Jamie Reid.

Jamie Reid got beaten up for wearing his own **GOD SAVE THE QUEEN** T-shirt and ended up with a broken nose and leg!

BAN THAT T

In Britain, T-shirts are liable to prosecution under the Indecent Displays (Control) Act 1981 and the Obscene Publications Act 1959 which make it an offence to 'publish' or publicly display indecent material.

T-shirts which The Metropolitan Police have taken action against include several featuring male genitals—Malcolm McLaren's T of two cowboys, naked from the waist down, was one.

Offensively rude slogans also qualify and a stall holder was fined £50 for selling a shirt which read: BEAT ME, BITE ME, WHIP ME, F**K ME LIKE THE DIRTY PIG I AM, COME ALL OVER MY TITS AND TELL ME THAT YOU LOVE ME, THEN GET THE F**K OUT!

WHO GIVES A F**K WHAT FRANKIE SAYS and F**K TO DANCING LET'S F**K also earned £50 fines; while Artificial Eye's T-shirts bearing pictures of notorious murderers Myra Hindley and Ian Brady were withdrawn from sale after Obscene Publications Squad Officers visited the shop.

These shirts caused public outcry in England as they featured sentences from a tape recording made while Hindley and Brady murdered one of their young victims. Meanwhile European Son's HITLER TOUR T-shirt generated a global furore.

Widely pirated, the design sold phenomenally round the world. Banned in Holland and Germany, it led to fights between British and German tourists at holiday resorts in Spain. In America, the Jewish Defence League apparently threatened to blow up the New York Bleeker Bob's record store unless they stopped stocking it, and several store windows were smashed after displaying it.

Above: European Son's 1981 3D T-shirt nasties in liquid latex.

Left: Sid Vicious wearing Malcolm McLaren's Cowboys shirt. The Sex Pistols frequently dressed in clothes from his shop.

Above (middle): Stiff Records' aggressive promo T.

Above: the classic slogan: Al McDowell's 1979 FUCK ART LET'S DANCE is still selling. Al started out working with Malcolm McLaren and went on to form State Arts.

song titles. GERMFREE ADOLESCENTS, one of the most successful, combined consumerist parody and photomontage, framing the band with household cleaning products.

The Boy shop in the Kings Road was one of the first to stock 'punk' T's, followed by small shops up and down the country. By 1978 orders were flooding in from America and Europe and demand was such that the shirts were selling almost before they had been printed. Ten years on, original British T-shirts continue to be international bestsellers, while Japan has become a major market.

Produced by small companies who trace their inspiration if not their roots back to punk, they sell their brands of subversion to followers of UK cult fashion. Wayne at European Son created a range of 10 uniquely offensive 3-D T's in 1981. CANCER featured cigarette butts and ash embedded in a liquid latex cross-section of a lung, while his MUMMY was made up of a melted doll's head, plastic fingers and used condoms in a pool of black and red latex!

European Son also printed shirts showing President Reagan made over to look like Hitler, with swastikas in place of the tradtional stars in the US flag. Another design saw President Kennedy smiling as gore exploded out of the side of his head. These last two both earned smashed-in shop windows in the States, but current British offerings are proving equally controversial.

London-based Artificial Eye have had to discontinue their George Cross shirt after accusations of catering for the neo-fascist market; while their SS soldier with the caption IS THIS WHAT THE GOVERNMENT IS COMING TO? outraged the *Jewish Chronicle*. They nonetheless continue to print T's like the MURDERERS range starring Charles Manson and the Reverend Jim Jones among others.

Without punk, such designs would not be possible, but its influences have been felt across the spectrum. By putting T-shirts under the spotlight, punk gave them credibility, inspiring the subsequent British art shirt boom and revitalizing conventional music T-shirt designs. Last but not least, the movement re-established the T-shirt as a way of getting up people's noses—in true Brando style!

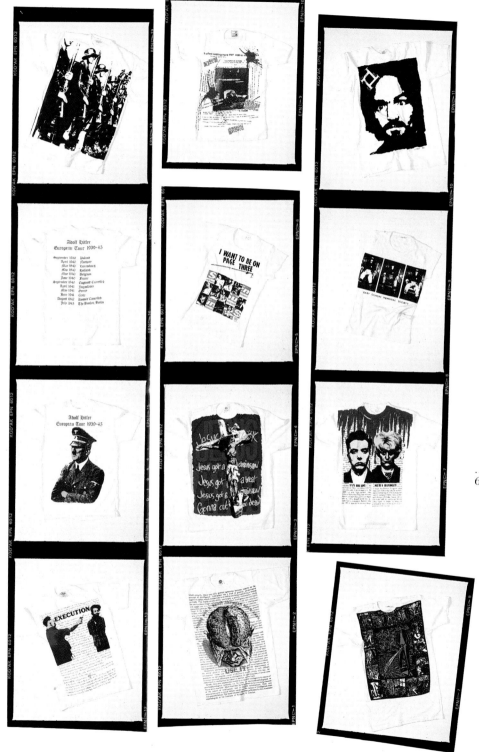

63

THE SIGN OF THE TRIBE

Lee Drummond, an anthropologist studying T-shirts at McGill University in Montreal, calls T-shirts the "new primitivism" and says they "take the stuff of our culture—a corporate consumer culture—and use that as a token of our identity."

T-shirts have become 20th century identity statements. Used to convey tribal and cultural allegiances, they serve the same function as Polynesian tattooing or South American Indian body painting. Shirts printed with team names represent the most straightforward identity garments, but the majority also feature evocative images which work as visual ciphers.

The Washington Bears and Princeton Tigers have traditional mascots, rock fans wear pictures of their bands or artwork from record sleeves. Bikers round the world share rebel patriot graphics and are the most committed ID shirt consumers. Marlon Brando wore a plain T to play Johnny, the "inarticulate leader of the Black Rebels Motorcycle Club" in the 1953 film *The Wild One*. Soon after, chapter and club names crossed over from jackets to T-shirts.

The film was based on the 1947 Hollister "riots" in California. What was actually just a wild weekend, was denounced by the press as the biggest threat to the American way of life since Pearl Harbour. Bikers were seen as outlaws and the image attracted men who had failed to fit in with conventional society. Early hardcore members were ex-GI's, now they are Viet Vets—and their T-shirts affirm a common identity.

Chapters function like old fraternities. Bikers live together, ride together and look after each other. They also wear the same shirts. AMERICAN BY BIRTH, REBEL BY CHOICE and UNTAMED LEGEND are universal slogans. Solidarity is very important and is expressed on everyting from shirts commemorating major biker events like Sturgis —bikers *always* buy a shirt to prove they were there—to the

An estimated 60–70 per cent of hardcore American bikers are Vietnam Veterans.

Below: a selection of mercenary T's.

64

Right: these all-American T's are popular with bikers and military personnel. They are produced by small companies like the Los Angeles Roger That Inc, who commissioned Lieutenant Tom Obleck to illustrate the I WAS KILLING WHEN KILLING WASN'T COOL shirt.

Standard T-shirt sizes go from small to extra large. 400lb bikers take theirs in JUMBO—XXL & XXXL.

Left: Artistique et Sentimentale's GLORY reworks the biker skull and flag ikons.

Left: bikers combine intense patriotism with a contempt for the more mundane aspects of the law and like their T-shirts to spell out their beliefs.

"Rugged men, who have an unconscious urge to express and reinforce their masculinity, used to have tattoos of women, daggers, snakes, dragons and the like. Now they wear T-shirts with beer cans, motorcycles, bullfighters or scenes of sporting events. It's the same thing." T-shirt designer, Frank Dunn.

Hells Angels Defence Fund T's.

Major graphic themes include eagles, bikers and their 'hogs', skulls, and grim reapers while swastikas and other Nazi symbols are also popular. Harley Davidson licensed T's sell in their millions but Harley fans also go for slogans like RIDING A HONDA IS LIKE FUCKING A FAGGOT. IT FEELS GOOD TIL SOMEONE YOU KNOW SEES YOU. 'Old ladies' wear MY OLD MAN RIDES THE BEST —HIS HARLEY AND ME or say they are SCOOTER FOXES.

American truckers, meanwhile, have taken to wearing their 18 wheelers on their chests. The trucks are set against epic scenery and dramatic skies and capped with all-American slogans like THE LAST FRONTIER and ON THE ROAD AGAIN. Truckers and bikers have their vehicles in common but identity T's are also worn by more loosely linked groups of people.

Time magazine's 1967 cover story described hippies as "internal emigres, seeking individual liberation through means as various as drug use [and] total withdrawal from the economy."

Extremists wanted to put LSD in the water supply and legal marijuhana was something all hippies agreed on, and

Not all identity T's are strictly serious as members of the NATIONAL ASSOCIATION OF AMATEUR GYNAECOLO-GISTS and LADIES SEWING CIRCLE & TERRORIST SOCIETY will testify.

Above: perverted patriotism: American White Power share the beliefs of the British National Front.

drugs became the common denominator for a very diverse movement. You may not have been able to smoke grass on the streets but wearing a VOTE YES or SMOKE COLUMBIAN T was the next best thing. The first "drug T's" surfaced in San Francisco and before long were being sold in headshops everywhere. Typical of the time is the 1973 BETTER LIVING THRU CHEMISTRY range whose trippy graphics promoted THC, LSD, MESCALINE, COCAINE & QUAALUDE.

1987 CALIFORNIAN HOMEGROWERS ASSOCIA-TION T's are more subtle. 'Brands' including MUY BLASTIDO ULTIMATE SINSE and STUPOR FARMS BUDS are presented in pastiche 40's style ads. Drugs are now seen as a private recreational activity rather than a public cause and these shirts are for committed consumers.

Elsewhere, subcultures from the New York subway vigilantes, the Guardian Angels, to the sinister Ku Klux Klan use T-shirts as instant IDs.

Mercenaries claim to DO IT FOR PROFIT, or boast TERRORISM STOPS HERE while the human catchment area for BEER LOVERS T's or slogan shirts like I'M ONLY HERE FOR THE BEER and I WISH YOU WERE A BEER is almost limitless . . .

Left: drugs have inspired T-shirt artists from R Crumb onwards.

Right: UK Today's shirts are tailor-made for youth tribes. Neofascists wore the George Cross T as a symbol of Britain's former power. Protests resulted in its discontinua-tion.

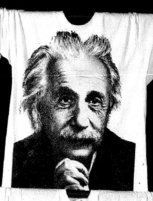

CHAPTER 12

WEARING YOUR HEROES

Left: *T-shirt tributes enshrine everything from cult TV serials to composers, along with pop and movie stars, and are the product of 50 years of evolution. American T's first featured cartoon characters and politicians in the 30's and 40's. Hero shirts only got going in the late 60's and early 70's, however, when rock fans started wearing their idols. The Jimi Hendrix and Ché Guevara T's are typical of the period.*

Wearing someone else's face on your chest has to be the ultimate form of hero worship and a major area of T-shirt culture is based on taking bedroom poster shrines out on the street. Heads and shoulders of larger-than-life legends fill up the whole shirt front while the rebel angle is a key selling point. Monroe, Dean, and Hendrix are among pop icons whose "live fast and die young" lifestyles have launched a million shirts.

The biggest stars are almost all dead or fictitious. Clint Eastwood and Sergeant Bilko are worn for their parts, not their personalities, and epic rôle models include political visionaries like Karl Marx, Ché Guevara and Martin Luther

An American department store asked European Son if they could print Jimi Hendrix's face any other color than brown in order to maximise sales to white fans . . .

King. Many are pictured with evocative accessories. Marilyn comes complete with pills in a frozen Warhol smile while Jesus Christ appears with a final crown of thorns.

Sid Vicious self-destructed, and his sordid death guaranteed him T-shirt immortality. One tribute to this 70's rebel without a cause shows him shooting up beside a scrawled tabloid epitaph which reads: SID THE FORMER SEX PISTOL, TOLD POLICE, "KILL ME MY BABY IS DEAD." LATER HE TOLD DETECTIVES "I STABBED HER BUT I DIDN'T MEAN TO KILL HER, I LOVED HER". ASKED WHY HE DID NOT HELP HER HE SAID "I AM A DOG".

Current media myths can also become T-shirt heroes. Aviator Mathias Rust achieved the impossible when he landed his Cessna in Moscow's Red Square. West Germans and Finns interpreted it as an act of defiance against their Eastern Block neighbours and rushed to buy INTERNATIONAL AIRPORT, RED SQURE, OPENING MAY 28, 1987 T-shirts. A young Finn explained their popularity to *The Times* newspaper saying: "For us, he is a real hero."

The text on Artistique et Sentimentale's Joy Division shirt reads as the perfect tribute to a dead hero: ON SATURDAY MAY 17, FOUR DAYS BEFORE JOY DIVISION WAS TO FLY TO AMERICA HE VISITED HIS OLD HOUSE IN MACCLESFIELD TO WATCH THE TELEVISED FILM 'STROSZEK' BY HIS FAVOURITE DIRECTOR 'HERZOG'. HOURS LATER, EARLY ON SUNDAY MORNING HE HUNG HIMSELF. HE WAS 23.

Above: **rock and pop icons fall into two categories—current and cult. The Duran Duran T is an example of the former and sold in huge quantities for as long as they remained in the charts. Cult heroes have a longer shelflife—demand for Ziggy Stardust and Jim Morrison T's being almost infinite . . .**

Above: **James Dean is another T-shirt perennial and it is likely that shops will still be stocking** **similar models when this particular T re-emerges from its time capsule.**

Left: the bigger the better: true fans can envelop themselves in images of their idols. Rock band The Tube created the first oversized face T's in the 70's, but it took ten years for the style to catch on in the massmarket.

71

Above: The King lives on— the 80's have seen a major revival in Elvis T's. The images are invariably from a time when he was still young and beautiful.

Right: Iggy Pop wears a shot of Jack Nicholson in *The Shining.*

Left and right: cartoon T's, originally for kids, became adult wear in the 60's— Disney and Warner characters blending perfectly with pop art and fantasy fashions. 80's shirts range from the hardcore styles of comics like *2000AD* and *Swamp Thing,* to re-runs of R Crumb characters.

CHAPTER 13

ART ON YOUR CHEST

Above and below: Softcell star Marc Almond in Artistique et Sentimentale's VOODOO T and their ART ON YOUR SLEEVE tribute to Mondrian.

In 1970 the Corcoran museum in Washington exhibited a sculpture made out of 500 white Fruit of The Loom T-shirts. It was probably the only instance in which a plain shirt has been perceived as a work of art. Printed shirts have seldom enjoyed similar recognition although many now feature graphics by practicing artists, who use the medium to make their work affordable and visible.

A product of the increasingly fine line between fashion and art, these T's range from signed originals to mass produced copies of artists' work and include shirts hand printed by, or under the supervision of, their designers in comparatively small runs. Designs are limited by what people will wear—abstract images do not sell well—and styles have to fit in with current fashions.

Museums have had a mixed response to the latest art medium. Californian galleries exhibit T-shirts, and the Institute of Contemporary Art in London showed them alongside avant-garde sculptures in 1981. The Victoria and Albert museum insisted that T-shirt designs be printed on cloth in order to be included in their 1974 Fabric of Pop exhibition, but the Detroit Institute of Arts took a more liberal attitude.

Their 1975 show, called quite simply The T-Shirt, was the first major T-shirt exhibition to be organized by a serious museum. It featured 200 models from 50's Little League memorabilia to rock, promotional and political shirts and attracted widespread press coverage. One reviewer wrote that it was "filled with mind-bending, chest-expanding images . . . the T-shirts are narrative visions of a cosmic lifestyle."

On New York's East 64th Street, Finn's T-shirt Gallery has been pulling in crowds since 1976. The Gallery celebrates T-shirt art in all its forms and opened with an exhibition of artist Peter Max's T's. A hand painted Max original went for $2.000, but could be considered a good investment, as his paintings were fetching up to $50,000 in 1987.

T-shirts by Andy Warhol, Jackson Pollock, Salvador Dali, Michael Konegan and Norris Burroughs come in signed, orginal overpainted prints and limited editions. Other gallery exhibitions have had themes ranging from Broadway shows to shirts designed by Latin artists and leading fashion illustrators. A "Britain Salutes America" special focused on British designers and 5,000 fans turned up to a T-shirt party show Finn organized at Studio 54.

Willi Smith, found of the Willi Wear fashion empire, launched his collection of T-shirts by contemporary American artists at Manhattan's fashionable Area club. A British series followed with shirts by Brian Clark, Gilbert and George and Patrick Caulfield among others. The Willi Wear range sells in clothes shops while art galleries stock T-shirts alongside posters and cards.

Cream Teas' "Designer Art" T-shirts by young artists sell round the world, as do Mile High Shirts' Ralph Steadman prints, but these types of art shirts are principally an 80's phenomenon. Hand painted hippy T's created the first wearable shirt art to go with embroidered jeans; while early mass production was organized by Haight Ashbury psychedelic poster supremos Mouse and Kelley.

Mouse and Kelley T-shirts including ZIG ZAG MAN, CALIFORNIA and the Grateful Dead series were sold through their mail order Monster company set up in 1971.

The official Soviet journal, *Young Communist*, ran an article in August 1985 denouncing T-shirts, along with rock music, as part of a propaganda campaign designed to incite anti-socialist opposition. Wearing a T-shirt was equated with blaspheming the Soviet state . . .

Right: a selection of John and Molly Dove's shirts: Leopardskin Girls ('74), Exploding Coke ('75), Jackson Pollock Tribute ('77), Last Kiss ('79) and Rock 'n' Roll Heart ('83).

Right: Earthly Delights: designs by eight UK illustrators were printed in limited editions of 100 for Christmas '85.

Left: Cream Tea was set up in 1986. Their high quality shirts feature the work of top young British artists and sell in upmarket fashion outlets round the world.

(Harry Truman - August 6, 1945)

'This is the greatest thing in history'

YES! N°

SOCIALISM

PEACE on EARTH, & lo, outspread
o'er the world the BANNER RED!

Left, right and below: Willi Wear's art shirt range, conceived by Willi Smith to gain a wider audience for the work of contemporary artists, was launched in America in '84 and Britain in '85.

Left: John and Molly Dove T's. Exploding Mickey was withdrawn after Disney objected.

The complex graphic style had been pioneered on dance hall posters and its transfer onto T's was made possible by revolutionary four-color printing.

Methods used to realize a design are crucial in a medium where the look of a print is dependent on very specific factors. T-shirts are printed by forcing ink through a partially blocked screen using a squedgee, and the end product is determined both by the type and gauge of screen mesh—organdie produces much sharper images than nylon, for instance,—and the angle and force with which the squedgee is pulled across the screen.

The process is largely automated with major commercial printers. Certain effects are only possible when shirts are printed by hand, however, and art T-shirts are often produced by small companies who use silkscreen techniques with the precision of a paint brush. One such is Modzart. Owners John and Molly Dove have been designing and printing T-shirts since 1969 and their consistently innovative style has been at the cutting edge of T-shirt graphics for the past two decades.

Their first collection of tattoo prints was snapped up by Bloomingdales, and subsequent outlets included the exclusive Paradise Garage and Granny Takes A Trip boutiques in London's Kings Road. The Doves started out mixing all their own inks and in 1970 worked out how to print on black T-shirts—commercially produced inks which did this only became available in 1975—and used the technique for the rhinestone studded WILD THING T.

Designed as a tribute to Jimi Hendrix, it featured a roaring leopard head with the words WILD THING underneath and was pirated from America to Brazil to become one of the first global T-shirt hits. Its success launched rhinestones as a major T-shirt fashion and by 1973 the Doves were selling thousands of shirts under their Wonder Workshop label.

Lou Reed, Mick Jagger, Marc Bolan and Paul McCartney were photographed in state of the art shirts like PIN UP GIRLS and MY BABY LOVES THE WESTERN MOVIES. A pioneering use of photomontage techniques for T-shirt graphics produced LIPS and LEOPARD GIRLS in 1974,

while the EXPLODING MICKEY T combined skilled draughtsmanship with explosive colors to evoke the American Dream gone berserk.

CHERISHED MEMORIES immortalized legends like Gene Vincent, Buddy Holly and James Dean and was followed in '79 by the REBEL COLLECTION. Elvis, Sid Vicious and Iggy Pop were among the chosen few and these tributes were the result of months of work. Other Dove classics include H-BOMB's nuclear kitsch graphics; while 80's output ranges from SMILE's surrealist letters and dreamy images to the precisely drawn CCCPUKUSA with its Union Jack, Hammer and Sickle and Stars and Stripes.

The Doves' Modzart shirts are exported round the world, and Artistique et Sentimentale are another British company whose distinctive T-shirt graphics have received international acclaim. Tony and Michelle designed their first shirt in the late 70's and their complex hand printed designs are now T-shirt classics.

Images ranging from cartoon characters and rococo cherubs to religious woodcuts are fused with literary texts and pop icons and condensed into uniquely intricate T-shirts. EAT THE RICH shows Fred Flintstone guzzling under a cartoon style CHOMP! CHEW! caption. Closer inspection reveals a detailed description of high-class cannibalism which opens with the words: "IT WAS A MAN'S RIGHT ARM . . ."

EVERYBODY HAS ROOTS is stamped across a classic Marilyn Monroe pose and the image is framed with the names of other notable dyed blondes. Siouxsie Sioux's face comes overprinted with a Swinburne quote and blackmail letters spell out HELL against a backdrop of medieval devils.

Anyone can reproduce a Picasso on a T-shirt but these two companies illustrate the way in which individual T-shirt artists are using a mass-produced garment as an alternative canvas. Genuine T-shirt art brings together flat design and print skills and turns them into a wearable, three dimensional experience. it also provides a new way of viewing conventional images and as such is a very exciting art medium.

Dr Dorothy Behling, assistant professor of merchandising (fashion) design and fashion theory at Bowling Green State University, conducted the first empirical study of T-shirts in 1986. Students were asked to place a pre-selected set of shirts in order of preference.

The top three categories were status T's, advertising T's and sporting T's. Dr Behling also observed graphic shirts had taken over from the slogan shirts of the 70's as the most popular style.

The average American owns more than six printed T-shirts. 66 per cent own at least one printed shirt.

Above: BLUE MAGIC (top left) and SEPPUKU! (top right) by Artistique et Sentimentale, whose complex T's can take months to research and design.

Right: John and Molly Dove T's: Pop Go The Easel ('83), Time to Laugh ('85), Anarchy Is ('83), Smile ('84), Too Hot To Handle ('84), Butterflies and Bullets ('85).

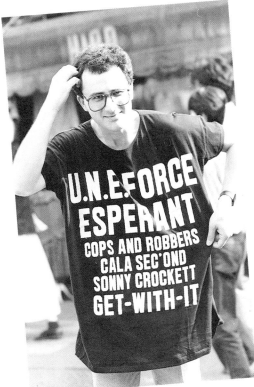

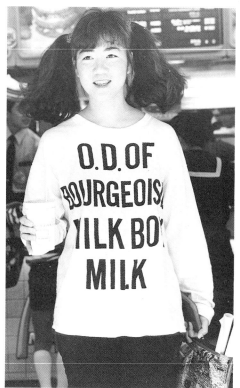

THE MEDIUM FOR THE MESSAGE

Above, above right and left: these revealing photos of Prince Andrew and Madonna were used in newspapers round the world. Top-selling Tokyo T's for 1987 were far more inscrutable, however.

Madonna's T-shirt said ITALIANS DO IT BETTER, Prince Andrew's claimed he was ALMOST FAMOUS and committed consumers wear WHOEVER SAYS MONEY CAN'T BUY HAPPINESS DOESN'T KNOW WHERE TO SHOP. Message shirts are the most direct form of T-shirt communication. Slogans crossed over from button badges to T's in the late 1950's and people have been advertising their attitudes on their shirt fronts ever since.

60's slogans promoted feminism or banned the bomb while Carnaby Street churned out light-hearted lines like I LOVE PAUL and READY STEADY GONK. Hippies had asked WHAT IF THEY HAD A WAR . . . AND NOBODY CAME?, and T-shirts became the perfect way of spelling out your support for everything from the equal rights movement to environmental pressure groups that followed in the 70's.

Serious shirts were in a minority, however, during a decade when looser fashions left people free to wear their feelings on their chests. *The New York Times* observed "The T-shirt has become the medium for a message" in August 1973. People who wanted to score points could buy KISS ME I DON'T SMOKE and WOMAN'S PLACE IS IN THE HOUSE AND SENATE, but most preferred lines like IF YOU FEEL SEXY SMILE.

HALLO SAILOR, POW! and KISS ME QUICK were other bestsellers, as was JOIN THE ARMY, TRAVEL TO EXOTIC DISTANT LANDS, MEET EXCITING UNUSUAL PEOPLE AND KILL THEM. Quirkier quotes included I SPENT MY VACATION AT THE GAS STATION and EAT AMERICAN FISH. 100 MILLION RUSSIANS CAN'T BE WRONG, while *Life Magazine* ran a tribute to talking T's in their summary of 70's styles.

"We try to have a good taste level, but we've got to stay economic." Marc Polish, the Philadelphia T-shirt Museum.

Left: England's entry into the Common Market and the Falklands War are just two of the issues on which T-shirt slogans attempted to influence public opinion.

Above: LETS SAVE LIVES ('85) and WORLDWIDE NUCLEAR BAN NOW ('84): two of Katharine Hamnett's slogan T-shirts. Inspiration for the campaigning style came from the 1983 Buddhist CHOOSE LIFE exhibition.

Right:
Katharine Hamnett and Margaret Thatcher at the Downing Street reception that unwittingly blasted her slogan style to instant stardom in March '84. Profits from the shirts were donated to the NSPCC.

The two page T-shirt feature was titled "We Wore Our Slogans On Our Chests" and the text stressed the importance of this new form of communication: "T-shirts in the 70's were no longer just underwear; they were compact, up-front, low-risk modes of self-expression. Of the 300 million loomed annually, one out of four had something to say about almost everything. Got the message?"

Non-verbal bombardment has continued to be a major feature of 80's T-shirts. Katharine Hamnett was photographed shaking hands with Mrs Thatcher in a 58% DON'T WANT PERSHING shirt in March 1984, and her pure protest T's turned slogans into designer fashion items overnight. Stark black letters fill up the 2ft by 3ft shirt front in what is the single strongest T-shirt style to emerge from the decade.

Unlike 70's frivolities, however, Hamnett messages are deadly serious. EDUCATION NOT MISSILES, STOP ACID RAIN, HEROIN FREE ZONE, and WORLDWIDE NUCLEAR BAN NOW combine the impact of tabloid headlines with the passion of a hell fire preacher. Hamnett explains her inspiration in equally uncompromising terms: "You feel you have to do something because the world's going to blow up, we're going to be poisoned or choked or gassed or virused to death."

82

"I thought I could get the generation who buy my clothes to think along the same lines as I do by having them wear a T-shirt that says STOP ACID RAIN" Katharine Hamnett.

Katharine Hamnett originally designed her giant slogans to be readable at contact picture size.

Left and opposite page: "They're designed so that wherever you see them you can read them. By the time you've actually finished reading the slogan it's too late, the message is already in your brain. It's designed to be subliminal . . . If the government won't represent the people, the people must represent themselves. And if they can't actually make a stand at least they can wear one." Katharine Hamnett, *Blueprint*, October '84.

83

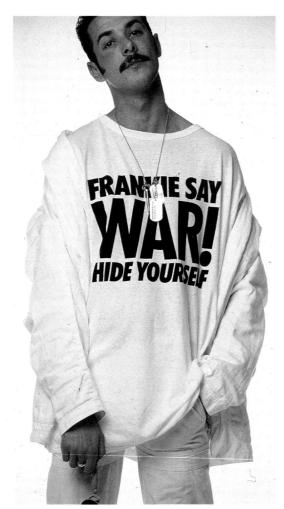

Left: Paul Rutherford of Frankie Goes To Hollywood.

Below: Frankie shirts were everywhere during the summer of '84 and T-shirt pirates made a killing ripping off the style.

RELAX
The unofficial Frankie

FRANKIE SAY ARM THE UNEMPLOYED
The official, radical Frankie

WOMEN ARE ANGRY
Radical, but not Frankie

KEEP THE G.L.C.
Just plain radical

STOP KILLING WAVES
Just plain confusing

STOP
Could be radical but it depends what with

BIG WORDS

BIG FUN
Short and to the point

START

Big words on even bigger t-shirts are definitely this summer's thing. In fact, seems like you can take any sail-sized singlet, bung some large black letters on it and (especially if it includes the legend 'Frankie say') someone'll want to wear it. Trendy designer Katherine Hamnett started all this off with a series of enormous tops emblazoned with anti-nuclear slogans (including the much copied 'Choose Life'). Said shirts were then seen dwarfing the torsos of everyone from Frankie to Wham! to Boy George. Frankie leapt straight on to the bandwagon with their own series and 'Relax' (again much imitated) became the word of the season. Meanwhile, every small clothes business in me (and) and many of the pop groups) begun bunging out their own variations. And here's a selection snapped in Carnaby Street.

HOT

BLACK LIFE
Short and to be worn with shorts

CHOOSE LIFE
The slogan that launched a thousand shirts (this is a copy, actually)

CHOOSE WHAM!
Rather have life, thank you

JUST SEVNTEEN
How did this get in here?

❻

Above: a page from *Smash Hits* magazine, summer '84.

BOW!

"A blank T-shirt! How trendy can you get?"

RELAX
TWO TRIBES

CHOOSE DEATH

I'M BARRY MANILOW'S MUM
FRANKIE SAY I'M BARRY MANILOW'S MUM

Left: Janet Street Porter in a homemade version of Hamnett's CHOOSE LIFE T.

Hamnett designed the style to be ripped off, and so spread the word, and the summer of '84 saw it hitting the streets on the back of the Frankie Goes To Hollywood phenomenon. *Relax* was at No. 1 in the charts and FRANKIE SAY prefaced commands from RELAX DON'T DO IT to ARM THE UNEMPLOYED and WAR! HIDE YOURSELF wherever you went. CHOOSE LIFE then became CHOOSE WHAM! while Sigue Sigue Sputnik T's said FLEECE THE WORLD and LET THEM KNOW IT'S SPUTNIK TIME in 1986.

Other 80's slogans are equally direct. BORN TO SHOP is just one of the 350 one-liners in stock at Marc Polish's Philadelphia T-Shirt Museum, where the bestsellers serve up humor spiked with flip cynicism. ALL THIS, AND BRAINS TOO came in at No. 1 in the Christmas '86 sales chart, while WHEN THE GOING GETS TOUGH, THE TOUGH GO SHOPPING and the classic BEAM ME UP SCOTTY . . . THERE'S NO INTELLIGENT LIFE HERE were second and third respectively.

Messages are designed to be taken in in the time it takes to read a shirt, and the rest of the Top Ten for '86 illustrate the style perfectly, ranging from I SURVIVED CATHOLIC SCHOOL to BECAUSE I'M THE DADDY, THAT'S WHY and WE'LL GET ALONG FINE AS SOON AS YOU REALISE I'M GOD.

More long-winded hits included INSANTITY IS HEREDITARY, YOU GET IT FROM YOUR CHILDREN; WHOEVER HAS THE MOST TOYS WHEN HE DIES, WINS and DON'T DRINK & DRIVE, YOU MIGHT HIT A BUMP AND SPILL YOUR DRINK.

English language slogans have also caught on in a big way in Japan, with the difference that the majority do not actually mean anything at all. Words are simply chosen because they look right and the result is shirts like the epic O.D. OF BOURGEOISIE MILK BOY MILK, PLEASURE SUPERPRESENT HISTRICDOLL KEEP OFF HISTRIC HOP GIRL, while the 1987 U.N.E. FORCE ESPERANT COPS AND ROBBERS CALA SEC'OND SONNY CROCKETT GET-WITH-IT is the shirt that says it all!

Right: slogan shirts gave cartoonists a field day, and this *Punch* cartoon by Michael Heath was just one of many commenting on the epidemic.

Below: Tony James of Sigue Sigue Sputnik. They had a substantial advance from EMI and extensive press coverage, but were thwarted in their attempt to FLEECE THE WORLD by the poor chart performance of their records.

THE SUN, Wednesday, September 26, 1984   3

WHO'S FRANKIE?

Beak in a pop quiz over girls in tease-shirts

By VAUGHAN FREEMAN

A magistrate asked in court yesterday who top pop group Frankie Goes to Hollywood were.

The bemused beak was swiftly told by prosecutor James Davis that the name "relates to a recent song in the hit parade."

The legal pop quiz happened as John Allison heard a case about saucy four-letter versions of the popular "Frankie says" T-shirts.

Helen Edmunds and Sandra Hurn, fans of Frankie and their singer Holly Johnson wore shirts with the slogan: "Frankie says —— me."

The girls, both 20, were arrested at a bus terminal after complaints, Mr. Davis told Swansea Magistrates.

Joke

Giggling Helen said the "tease-shirts" which they had done at a local...

Holly . . . front man of Frankie

The Philadelphia T-shirt Museum have sold over 100,000 PSYCHOTIC STATE T-shirts.

85

CHAPTER 15

COUTURE COTTON

"T-shirts are an inexpensive way of creating young high fashion and affordable designs. They are now in everybody's wardrobe." Jeffrey Rogers, whose company sells 5 million fashion shirts annually.

The term T-shirt entered the American vocabulary in 1944 according to *Webster's Dictionary*, and was used to define the white T-shaped serviceman's undershirt. Back then they cost around 50c. In 1987 the average price for a printed, color T-shirt was $10 while Ralph Lauren's silk couture versions retailed at £147. Between these dates and prices lies the story of the T-shirt's transition from undervest through novelty and anti-fashion to mainstream fashion item.

The late 50's saw the first non-underwear T-shirts. Plain models had become accepted male casual wear thanks to Marlon Brando and James Dean while the Beatniks

launched the first major T-shirt fashion with their blue and white striped matelot T. Printed and colored shirts and styles other than the box cut crewneck classic were still very rare, however, and only started to take off in the 1960's through the small boutiques.

London had given America the Beatles and the mini and its booming fashion scene provided the perfect springboard for the fashion T. Designers started experimenting with cotton jersey alongside the more outrageous PVC, lurex and ciré fabrics. The results ranged from T-shirt mini dresses to the three button grandpa vest, while decorative motifs included Michael English's pop art designs and Michael Rogers' satin appliquéd rockets and ice-cream cones.

Classic T's were jazzed up with contrasting collars and cuffs or worn sleeveless as the top half of flared cotton jersey pant suits. Long sleeved and skin tight, they became the

Time **magazine noted that the average retail price of T-shirts in 1970 was between $6–$12, although some were considerably cheaper.**

The Shimmy Like My Sister Kate fringed style and Chantilly Lace look were just two of 26 "Cheap but Chic" ways of customizing the basic T in the 1977 book *Tricks for T's*.

Right: **kids started wearing printed T-shirts in America in the 40's and 50's, long before they became accepted adult wear, and have stuck with the style ever since.**

Left and oposite page, top: **onetime Sex Pistol Steve Jones in a classic early 70's T, while Lulu and Jagger model the Breton or Matelot striped T. Brigitte Bardot and James Dean wore them, and the look has been a fashion favorite ever since the Beatniks popularised it in the 50's.**

backdrop for an explosion of fun images via Mr Freedom in the Kings Road. The boutique boldly took the T-shirt where no T-shirt had been before and their "popscenic wonderlands" were worn by everyone from Elton John to fashion models.

By the summer of 1970 Freedom's fantasy graphics were all the rage as Nova's Caroline Baker noted: "It's not only the Walt Disney characters that are making a cartoon-crazy fashion world—it's any pop symbol reminiscent of our times. In the Fifties—Elvis, ice-cream soda; further back into our childhood—boats and planes and clouds and sunbursts and, bringing us right back into the Seventies, Appollo rockets zooming all over us."

T-shirts were also "breaking out" in America according to *Time* magazine: "Suddenly this summer, the undershirt is very much back in—but not as an undergarment. Violently colored and decorated with cartoon characters, symbols of dissent or simple slogans, the shirts are a bright new trend for the kids—and the Over-30's too." *Vogue* took the line that "Art Can Be A Wearing Business" in 1971, and used T-shirts by Elizabeth Frink, David Hockney, Allen Jones and Patrick Hughes to prove their point.

Meanwhile hemlines were heading back down. *Rave* introduced the new T-shirt maxi dresses with the headline "Keep Your Shirt On . . . And On . . . And On" and enthused: "Look what's happened to T-shirts! They've

Karl Lagerfeld's official No. 5 and Chanel T-shirts sold out in London and Paris in 1987.

Opposite page: custom shirts: knotting and shredding are DIY techniques used to create variations on the basic T shape. Designers often have shirts made to complement their artwork, as with these longsleeved T's by the Doves.

Left: the T-shirt is essentially a blank canvas and fashion graphics mirror trends in popular culture from African art to jazz and hip hop.

Below and far right: the fashion slogan: VIVE and MUSCLE T's, designed by Trevor Miles for Tomboy, became massive 80's hits.

Above right (middle): Malcolm McLaren and Vivienne Westwood's tribal tube T was one of their post-punk experiments with the basic T shape.

Left (top to bottom): T-shirts by Tomboy, photographer Johnny Rosza, and Tim Shirts illustrate the variety of 80's styles.

The first colored T-shirts were pale blue models which came with pockets. By the early 70's the major mills had responded to public demand and were producing a wider range of colored T-shirts.

grown longer. This time last year the boys were all wearing these skin-tight vests. We spotted their possibilities and now the rag trade has transformed that dull old white vest into a lovely dress. Suits us to a T!"

Maxi shirts sported everything from Toulouse Lautrec prints to pop art appliqués and hand-painted flowers, but the short shirt scene was equally dynamic. Designer Anthony Price's cap sleeve style sold by the million, as did Virginia Anderson and Mary Anne Wyman's Cloud shirt, Trevor Miles' star signs, and the Doves' WILD THING tribute to Hendrix. The last three also shared the dubious honor of being the first original designs to be widely pirated.

The T-shirt revolution had become a sartorial gold rush. High street chain stores were beginning to move in but the majority of shirts still came from independent entrepreneurs. Glam ruled and the generation that wore 5 inch platforms with glitter sox also snapped up T-shirts that sparkled with sequins and rhinestones, came feathered or flocked with pink pussies, were laced to the waist and fringed round the sleeves, or studded with metal hearts and stars.

Fashion was "being able to wear spots with stripes, colors that clash, knickers that show" and the early 70's also saw the first mass-produced colored T's in shades from maroon and tangerine to cerise and lime green. Necklines were round, square, scooped or V-shaped, drawstrings finished off bell sleeves and women's shirts were cut out of pre-printed jersey whose all-over patterns ranged from candy-colored ice-cream cones to maps of Vietnam and Camel cigarette logos.

Such excesses were too over the top to last and the subsequent return to more casual dress styles, combined with the increasing popularity of sports clothes like baseball jackets and, later, track suits, saw the classic T-shape making a fashion comeback. Union Underwear's Fruit of The Loom logo and the American Farrah Fawcett transfers were the two major 'hits' of '76 and both came on straight box cut crewneck shirts.

Vogue had called jeans and T-shirts "the teenager's second skin protest against dressing" in 1975. The same

The first specialist trade magazines for T-shirts and imprinted sportswear started up in 1977.

Left: T's by Robin Richards *(far left)* and Alex McDowell's State Arts.

Right: the 80's have seen designers from Karl Lagerfeld to Paul Smith moving into T's. This selection of upmarket T's includes designs by: *(clockwise from top left)* John Lys Turner, Paul Smith, John Lys Turner, Tomboy, Huntley Muir, Art-O-Matic, Simon Pepper and The Cloth *(center).*

New for 1987: The Tee-Kini consisting of briefs for topless sunbathing and a matching cover-up T-shirt.

year saw them showing a David Bailey photo of Marie Helvin in an Yves St Laurent suit and fine striped T. Status seekers could meanwhile buy $14 shirts emblazoned with HARPER'S BAZAAR, ELLE and BIBA. This juxtaposition of straight style and street style, established in the 70's, has remained a major feature of 80's T-shirt fashions.

High street chains now employ full-time T-shirt designers and cotton jersey is reworked each season in much the same way as socks and hosiery. Color and cut change to fit in with the overall look but the 80's have also seen an increasing number of upmarket printed fashion T's. Punk graphics paved the way while the big baggy shirts introduced in the late 70's provided the canvas for a larger design.

Katharine Hamnett gave XXXL shape designer credibility when she used it as the billboard for her sartorial propaganda. The loose look has gone on to dominate the decade in which T-shirts have cast off their novelty image to become a serious fashion. *Elle* magazine raved about T-shirt mania and called them the "undisputed stars of the summer" (of '87) in just one of many tributes to a medium the fashion press had previously been reluctant to devote much space to.

This new-found appreciation stems partly from the T-shirt's increasingly high-class image. Paul Smith's upmarket prints have been sold round the world since 1983, as have those of retailer and style king Joseph Ettedgui. Joseph commissions his summer collections from cartoonists and artists, and his collaboration with Michael Roberts produced distinctive African inspired primitive art graphics and acid colored tributes to surfer style.

Photographer Bruce Weber's moody black and white pictures have also been transferred onto T's while The Cloth have had major success with their fine art shirts. The company was set up in 1983 by four Royal College of Art graduates to produce textiles evolved from their paintings and woodcuts and their strong pictorial images from Picassoesque birds to classic nudes have been widely copied.

Such shirts are essentially small run high fashion items.

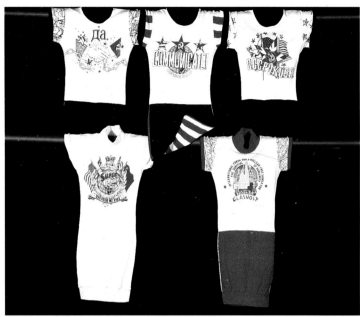

Above and below: The Cloth's annual Christmas T's are a designer first, while Smash's 11-color print is one of the most complex shirts on general sale.

Right: Russian graphics first featured on British T's in '77 and a decade later hit the highstreets against a background of Gorbachev's Glasnost, summits and arms talks.

Left: Russian T's for 1987 are the latest example of dressing for supremacy—or how powerful nations influence wardrobes round the world. American style T's, usually sporting or college, have been selling in Britain since the 70's while Japanese samurai and rising suns were very popular in the early '80's.

9–11 May 1978: The first trade show for T-shirts and imprinted sportswear was held in Dallas.

Less exclusive 80's styles range from the million-selling flag shirts popularised by Def Leppard in America to the 1987 US tie-die revival inspired partly by the Grateful Dead's tour. FRANKIE SAYS was everywhere in 1984, while in England Japanese samurai warriors and Russian revolutionary graphics reigned supreme for a season.

Pirate versions of designer logos—Gucci as Ducci, Chanel as Channel—defied the wrath of corporate lawyers. Cartoon characters from 2000 AD's Judge Dredd to the classic Mickey Mouse became born again bestsellers. New American entries into the comic folklore included Bad Dog and Spuds Mackenzie. The AIDS virus inspired T-shirts from Katharine Hamnett's FRANKIE SAYS WEAR A CONDOM to the FASHION CARES fundraiser.

Crazes come and go but the T-shirt's ability to react instantly to the latest trends has turned the one-time undervest into a fashion classic whose built-in obsolescence ensures it remains totally current. T-shirts are also infinitely versatile. *Elle* showed readers how to twist them into shorts. Other variations are shredded, knotted, draped or rolled, but whichever way you wear them, it seems the public can never get enough . . .

Fashion Weekly reported in May '87 that "demand for one of the season's hottest fashion items currently outstrips supply by 5 to 1—and already there are rumours of black market trading." Their headline story detailed a baggy "T-SHIRT FAMINE" in which Union Underwear revealed that even they were experiencing difficulty in obtaining enough cotton yarn and were planning to set up a new factory to cope with the demand.

By the late 80's major American mills were devoting 80 per cent of their output to colored shirts, while screen printers reported that turnover had increased by anthing from 20-40 per cent between 1986–7 alone. T-shirts fit all shapes and sizes and the undervest which gave body language a new meaning has become universal top wear. Designed as a throwaway, it nonetheless provides a unique record of 20th century popular culture. As the ultimate people's garment, the T-shirt is a story that will run and run . . .

ACKNOWLEDGEMENTS

The publishers would like to thank the following:

Adidas; Michael Adler; African National Congress; Alder Sportswear; American Silkscreen; Anheuser-Busch; The Anti Apartheid Movement; Artificial Eye; Artistique et Sentimentale; Associated Press; Assorted Images; The Athletic Supporter Ltd; David Austin; Beebs; Robin Beeche; Dorothy Behling Ph.D; The British Film Institute; The British Clothing Industry Association Ltd; The British Library; Marcia Byfield; Camerapix; Campaign for Nuclear Disarmament; Carraun Group plc; Chelsea Girl; Clones; The Cloth; The Coca-Cola Company; Coco; Colorific; *Company*; The Conservative Party; *Cosmopolitan*; Cream Tea; *Daily Mirror*; The Daily Telegraph Colour Library; David Mann Originals; The Detroit Institute of Arts; John and Molly Dove; Duke University; Alan Elenson; Electric Blue; *The Face*; Falcon Holidays; Fans; Fifth Column; Finn, The T-Shirt Gallery; Fleishmann Hillard Inc; Fotobank; Frank Spooner Pictures; Piers Golden, Life Products; The Great British T-Shirt Company; Greenpeace; Gregg Evans; Susan Griggs Agency Ltd; Guinness Brewing; Hanes Printables; Derek Hatton; Healthilife Ltd; Michael Heath; Alan Holden; The Home Office; IDAF; Illusion Enterprises; The Image Bank; Impact Photos; *Impressions Magazine*; Indiana University; In-Wear Matinique; Ira Sokoloff, Great Southern Company; Island Trading; Jamaican Tourist Board; Tom Johnston; *Just Seventeen*; Nick Knight; Las Vegas Convention and Visitors Authority; David Lavender; Levi Strauss UK Ltd; London Express; London Features International; Lonsdale Sports Equipment Ltd; Lynne Franks PR; McBlue; Tony McGee; Malcom McLaren; Media Merchandisers; Mile High Shirts; Trevor Miles; The Milk Marketing Board; Mobile Merchandising Company; Norma Moriceau; Dennis Morris, Epoch Productions Ltd; Jeffrey Morris; *Music Week*; National Council for Civil Liberties; Naval Historical Center; Northern Sun Merchandising; Ocean Pacific; *Oui*; David O'Keefe, Rock Tops; Outer Limits T-Shirt Company; *Outlaw Biker Magazine*; Louis Parker, Concorde; Pasiano Products; People in Pictures; Philadelphia T-Shirt Museum; *Photo*; Pictorial Press; Picture Bank; Pictures Colour Library; The Picture Library; *Point of Sale and Screen Printing*; Popperfoto; *Punch*; Jamie Reid; Robin Richards; Jeffrey Rogers; Roger That Inc; Gordon Savage, Mainline Promotions Ltd; *Screen Printing Magazine*; Sefton; Skies Photo Library; Smash; *Smash Hits*; Solo Syndication Literary Agency Ltd; Spectrum; Splash; Square Peg; Star Prints; *The Sun*; *The Sunday Times Magazine*; Sunshine Designs; Survivor Silk Screen Printing; Syndication International; Textile Market Studies; Things (Fashions) Ltd; 3D Emblem Corporation; Time-Life Library; Tom Boy; Tony Stone Worldwide; Topham; Transfer Images; Trog; Tronseal Ltd; Penny Tweedie; UCLA; Union Underwear Company Inc; University of Illinois; University of Michigan; University of Rochester; US Army Quartermaster Museum; Victoria and Albert Museum (Textile Department); Washington University; Wayne, European Son; Vivienne Westwood; Wide Eyed; Willi Wear; Winterland; John Withers; Nicholas Wolfers; Zefa.

The publishers would also like to thank anyone else who generously donated or loaned T-shirts for use in this book.